2/97

Settlement
in Missouri

WITHDRAWN

Project Sponsors

Missouri Center for the Book
Western Historical Manuscript Collection,
University of Missouri–Columbia

Consultant

Donald M. Lance

Special Thanks

Susanna Alexander
A. E. Schroeder
Paul Szopa, Academic Support Center,
University of Missouri–Columbia

Missouri Heritage Readers

General Editor, Rebecca B. Schroeder

Each Missouri Heritage Reader explores a particular aspect of the state's rich cultural heritage. Focusing on people, places, historical events, and the details of daily life, these books illustrate the ways in which people from all parts of the world contributed to the development of the state and the region. The books incorporate documentary and oral history, folklore, and informal literature in a way that makes these resources accessible to all Missourians.

Intended primarily for adult new readers, these books will also be invaluable to readers of all ages interested in the cultural and social history of Missouri.

Books in the Series

German Settlement in Missouri

New Land, Old Ways

*Robyn Burnett
and Ken Luebbering*

University of Missouri Press
Columbia and London

Library of Congress Cataloging-in-Publication Data

Burnett, Robyn.
    German settlement in Missouri : new land, old ways / Robyn
    Burnett and Ken Luebbering.
        p.   cm.—(Missouri heritage readers)
    Includes bibliographical references and index.
    ISBN 0-8262-1094-5 (alk. paper)
    1. German Americans—Missouri—History—19th century.
    2. Missouri—Emigration and immigration—History—19th cen-
    tury.   3. Readers for new literates.   I. Luebbering, Ken, 1946–
    II. Title.   III. Series.
    F475.G3B87   1996
    977.8'00431—dc20   96-42063
                                                                  CIP

∞ ™ This paper meets the requirements of the
American National Standard for Permanence of Paper
for Printed Library Materials, Z39.48, 1984.

Typesetter: BOOKCOMP
Printer and binder: Thomson-Shore, Inc.
Typefaces: Palatino and Bodoni

This book is dedicated to the immigrants who came . . .

from Bavaria, the Rhineland, and Westphalia,
    Hanover, Holstein, Saxony, and Silesia,
from Switzerland and Austria,
from Bohemia, Slovakia, and Poland,
from Italy, Greece, and France,
from Scotland, Ireland, and Wales,
from Ghana, Nigeria, and Kenya,
from Vietnam, Korea, and Thailand,
from Mexico, El Salvador, and Guatemala . . .

and to those who continue to come.

Contents

Acknowledgments

We want to thank all those who helped with this project. We owe a particular debt to Adolf E. Schroeder for his kindness, guidance, and willingness to share photographic and other materials in his collection. Randy Roberts helped us to identify the relevant collections at the Western Historical Manuscript Collection, and he and other staff cheerfully assisted us throughout the research process and in locating photographs. The staff at the State Historical Society of Missouri, Columbia, provided valuable assistance, especially Fae Sotham. Thank you also to the staffs at the Missouri Historical Society, the Missouri State Archives, the Jesuit Missouri Province Archives, and the Missouri Department of Natural Resources for their help.

German
Settlement
in Missouri

1

Introduction

The small houses, vineyards and livestock on the
steep hillsides overlooking the Missouri River need
only castles to remind one of . . . Germany.
  —Malcolm C. Drummond,
    Historic Sites in St. Charles County Missouri

Throughout its history the Missouri River Valley has been
a major pathway. Native Americans lived in villages along its
banks and followed the river on hunting trips. European settlement in the valley began with the coming of the French traders
in the eighteenth century. They used the river for carrying trade
goods west and bringing cargoes of furs down from the Rocky
Mountains and high plains.

Daniel Boone's arrival in Missouri in 1799 marked the beginning of a new era in America's westward push. In that same year,
twenty German and Swiss Lutheran and Mennonite families left
North Carolina to move to the western frontier. On January 1,
1800, they became the first group of German-speaking immigrants to cross the Mississippi River and settle in Missouri. They
built their homes along the White Water River in southeast Missouri in an area that is now a part of Cape Girardeau and Bollinger
Counties. One of the settlers, George Christopher Niswonger,
was 108 years old when he moved to Missouri. Missionary Tim-
othy Flint, who visited the community in 1819, reported that the
White Water River settlers were good farmers and self-sufficient.
In his *Recollections of the Last Ten Years . . . in the Valley of the Mississippi* he wrote, "I counted forty-five female dresses hung around
my sleeping-room, all from cotton raised, and manufactured, and
colored in the family."

Great waves of German immigrants came to America between 1815 and 1860. Most immigrants left home for two main

reasons: opportunities in the New World, and political and economic problems in Europe. People in the German states faced terrible hardships because of the costly wars against Napoleon, and many came to the United States to rebuild their lives.

One of the earliest Germans to visit Missouri, Gottfried Duden, wrote a book praising the land, waterways, and climate of the state. Partly because of Duden's book, Missouri became a popular destination for German immigrants; by 1860 more than half of Missouri's foreign-born residents were German.

The German immigrants who settled in Missouri included farmers, craftsmen, merchants, and professionals such as doctors and lawyers. Most came as individuals or single families, but some came with the help of settlement societies formed either in Germany or the eastern United States. The German Settlement Society of Philadelphia, for example, founded the city of Hermann.

German immigrants continued to settle in the Missouri River Valley and along the Osage and Gasconade Rivers throughout the nineteenth century. This area attracted so many Germans partly because it reminded them of the river valleys, forests, and hills of their homeland. It also provided rivers for transportation, fertile valleys for farming, forests for hunting, and hills for vineyards and orchards.

Large numbers of German immigrants made their homes in the lands along the Missouri River between St. Louis and Jefferson City. Others bought farms and formed communities away from the river in areas such as Bethel in Shelby County, Concordia in Lafayette County, and Cole Camp in Benton County. Wherever they founded communities, the Germans and their descendants maintained their building styles, language, and customs for several generations.

Immigrants who settled in towns with large American populations gave up their customs and language more quickly, but still contributed skills, knowledge, and cultural traditions to their new neighbors.

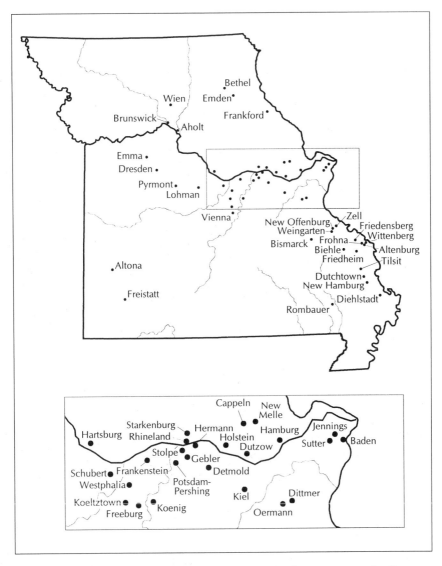

The Missouri towns with German names show where many early German immigrants to Missouri settled. Others settled in towns already established by Americans. (Mark Davis, GIS/RS Lab, Lincoln University, based on a map by Andreas Grotewald and Walter Schroeder, Geography Department, University of Missouri–Columbia)

2

Life in Germany

In the still seclusion of the Missouri forests, where nature still reigns supreme, there it must be better. There many hearts shaken by storms will find peace.

—Friedrich Steines,
Letter, April 1834

In the early 1800s there was no country called Germany. Instead there were about three hundred provinces and principalities ruled by kings, dukes, princes, or bishops. The French Revolution, which began in 1789, plunged Europe into a series of wars that lasted for twenty-five years. Napoleon, the French leader, tried to take over many other European countries. He was finally defeated in 1815. When the wars ended, the number of German states was reduced to about fifty.

Life was hard for the Germans who lived in these times. In some areas crops, livestock, and homes were destroyed in the wars, and many people lost their lives. Many Germans were poor and unemployed. Rural areas became too crowded for the land to provide a living.

Often farm families worked as weavers of linen cloth to add to their family's income. In the 1830s and 1840s, however, machines were invented to weave cotton cloth, and many German linen weavers lost their jobs. In addition, there were crop failures. In the 1830s the summers were cold and wet. The flax crops, from which linen is made, failed three years in a row, also causing a loss of jobs. Then in 1845, the potato crop in Germany was destroyed by the same disease that destroyed the Irish potato crop. In both countries, people starved.

There were political problems, too. Taxes were high to support the armies and the lives of the wealthy people. Religious practices were controlled by the government, and most political

4

Even after the Napoleonic Wars, the area we now call Germany included about fifty separate states. (A. E. Schroeder Collection, Western Historical Manuscript Collection–Columbia, courtesy of Walter Schroeder)

activity was forbidden. Men were forced to serve in the military. Revolutions and attempts to unify the German states failed; rulers imposed new restrictions in order to keep their power and wealth. Some people said that the only free Germans were in America or in their graves.

Because of the economic hardships and political turmoil they suffered, many Germans became interested in leaving home, especially when they heard of the opportunities in America. They were attracted by stories of cheap land, available jobs, low taxes, and political and religious freedom. Over the next fifty years, millions of Germans came to live in the United States.

3

German Books about Missouri

There is still room for millions of farms along the Missouri.
　　　　　—Gottfried Duden,
　　　　　Report on a Journey to the Western States of North America

[Many Germans] regret the day and hour when their eyes and their fancies were captivated by Duden's fallacious accounts of America.
　　　　　—Frederick Julius Gustorf,
　　　　　The Uncorrupted Heart

Groups of Germans had settled in the eastern United States beginning in 1683 when Germantown, Pennsylvania, was established. Pennsylvania, Maryland, Virginia, the Carolinas, and other states continued to attract large numbers of German immigrants.

When the United States purchased the Louisiana Territory from France in 1803, a vast new region opened up for settlement. This included the area that would later become the state of Missouri. However, at that time, few Europeans were coming to America because of the Napoleonic Wars. The end of the wars in 1815 allowed emigration to begin again.

In the 1820s a Prussian lawyer named Gottfried Duden came to believe that the only solution to the problems faced by the German people was to move to North America. Duden came to St. Louis with his friend Ludwig Eversmann in 1824 to look for a good location for large German settlements. He wanted to write a guide for Germans interested in coming to the United States.

Duden and Eversmann bought farms in what is now Warren County, about fifty miles west of St. Louis. Duden hired Americans to clear his land, build his cabin and fences, plant his crops, and hunt game for him. This allowed him to spend time reading, exploring the countryside, visiting his American neighbors, and writing letters. He lived on his farm for almost three years while he wrote a series of letters describing the opportunities available along the Missouri River.

Unfortunately for those who followed him, Missouri had mild winters and pleasant summers during the three years Duden lived on his farm. He warned readers about the problems of adapting to a different climate, the hardships of daily life, and homesickness, but his glowing descriptions of the beautiful countryside and free or cheap land in Missouri got the most attention.

Duden dreamed of a new Germany in the New World. "How often I have thought of the poor people of Germany," he wrote. "What abundance and success the industry of a few hands could bring to whole families."

Duden returned to Germany in 1827 and published his report of life in Missouri in 1829. Some fifty books about America were published in Germany between 1815 and 1848, but Duden's was probably read by the most people. His book brought thousands of people to Missouri. Although prosperous Germans were attracted by his report, Missouri must have sounded like paradise to the poor, crowded on worn-out land or with no land at all. In Germany they were taxed and persecuted by corrupt rulers, but life in Missouri promised freedom and a better future for their children.

One early German immigrant to Missouri who had read Duden's book was Nicholas Hesse. He had served as a minor government official in Prussia and found himself in some legal trouble. Hesse believed America was a land of opportunity where he could find a better life, but his experience here was very different from Duden's.

Hesse settled with his wife and six daughters in the isolated Westphalia settlement on the Maries River in present-day Osage County in 1835. He could not find people to do his work for him, as Duden did. The helpers who had come with him from

Nicholas Hesse did not find life in the new Westphalia settlement better than his life in Germany, but his book about the problems immigrants faced in Missouri did not discourage many other Germans from coming. (A. E. Schroeder Collection, Western Historical Manuscript Collection–Columbia)

Prussia soon left for better jobs. He was not used to the hard labor required on a farm, and his life did not seem better to him.

His wife was unhappy from the beginning. She was lonely on their farm and unable to cope with her separation from family and friends in Germany. Hesse and his family stayed in Missouri less than two years. When they returned to Germany, he wrote a book intended to correct Duden's optimism. "The longing for relatives, friends, and old acquaintances often brought a melancholy that could not be cured by any medicine," he wrote. The problems described in Hesse's book had little effect on Germans who had caught the "fever" to emigrate.

4

Emigration Fever

Let us build cabins on the Missouri
Where the sun of freedom shines.
—Friedrich Muench,
"Emigration Song"

For a time everyone in the German states must have been talking of opportunities across the Atlantic in America. Many books, like Gottfried Duden's, gave glowing accounts of life in the new territories west of the Mississippi. Many who learned of America from books got helpful advice, but much was impractical. Writers like Duden or even Nicholas Hesse, who were only in America for a few years, sometimes did not know as much as emigrants needed to know about life on the frontier.

Duden's book was only one of the reasons for the massive German emigration to Missouri during the next three decades. The letters written home by the ordinary farmers and laborers about their successes in St. Louis, or Augusta, or Westphalia, were even more important. The letters created so much interest in emigrating to America that some government officials in the German states worried that too many people would leave. They tried to spread information about problems Germans would face in the new country, but the proud reports of success friends and relatives found in America proved too powerful.

It is mainly because of the letters home that many communities in Missouri were settled by emigrants from a single area in Germany. In Osage County, for example, Westphalia was settled mostly by persons coming from the province of Westphalia in Germany. Loose Creek became home to those from the Lower Rhine Valley, while Rich Fountain's families came mostly from Bavaria. Villagers near Osnabrück, Germany, knew from letters home that people from their region had gone to Washington, Missouri; others followed and bought land near them. Emigrants from Hanover settled Concordia in western Missouri, following early English-speaking pioneers to the area.

Many who left Germany were farmworkers who were too poor to own land. In Germany they had little that was their own besides their clothes and perhaps a few farm animals. Often a single hog butchered during the winter provided the only meat for the year. They worked long days, frequently at no pay, for the wealthier peasants or nobles who owned the land. At home, they had no hope of things getting better.

The letters that friends and relatives sent back from America told of a much different life. After only three or four years immigrants owned forty or even eighty acres of land. They had built a log house at least as good as the one they left in their old village. They owned a team of horses, milked several cows, and ate meat every day.

One letter to relatives still living in the Rhine Valley contained a song describing the feelings of many immigrants in America:

> Hail Columbus, praise to thee . . .
> Thou hast shown to us the way
> Out of our hard servitude,
> To save us, if we only dare
> To bid our Fatherland farewell.

Once the family in Germany read these letters from America, of course, they showed them all around the village, proud of the success their relative had found. Those left in the village could see that life was not getting better for themselves, and many soon made plans to join their friends in America.

One German wrote a poem that shows the impression such letters made.

> My cousin wrote me just a while ago
>   from this beautiful land
> And I really won't stay here much longer,
>   I want to go to the beautiful land.
> Raisins, almonds are eaten there
>   as in this country one eats bread
> For in the land of America there is no want.

These two drawings made in Germany in 1838 show the contrast between the paradise that some Germans believed they would find in America and the reality of the hard work that awaited them. (A. E. Schroeder Collection, Western Historical Manuscript Collection–Columbia, courtesy of Countess von Lippe, Institute for Foreign Relations—Stuttgart)

Once a person decided to emigrate, the fever often spread quickly to other family members. The Wallenkamp family is one example. Henry Wallenkamp was born in Osnabrück in 1822. His father owned a large farm and a tile factory. When Henry was fourteen his mother died suddenly. The family was devastated. Knowing others who had gone to America, Henry's older brother made up his mind to emigrate.

His father soon decided to follow. When he offered his farm and business for sale, his neighbors were shocked that such a prosperous businessman was leaving. Two of Wallenkamp's sisters and their husbands decided to accompany him. When they departed a year later, there were 110 people in the group that left Osnabrück for Washington in Franklin County, Missouri.

Because of this "emigration fever," Germans came to America in waves. In the 1820s only about 8,000 emigrants came. After the publication of the books by Duden and others and the letters from America, that small trickle became a flood. In the 1830s, more than 150,000 Germans arrived in America. In the next decade almost three times that many came, with 100,000 arriving in 1847 alone.

Democratic revolutions throughout the German states in 1848 failed, and serious economic problems increased. More than half a million Germans left their homes between 1850 and 1854, with an equal number leaving during the rest of the decade. Emigration slowed during the 1860s, probably more because of the Civil War in the United States than because of improvements in Germany. It increased again following the formation of the German Empire in 1871. More than a million and a half people emigrated between 1870 and the mid-1880s. In all, more than seven million came to the United States from German-speaking lands.

5

The Atlantic Voyage:
Floating Coffins

Bremen is the gathering place for a large part of the emigrants from many regions of Germany. There many walk about in the foretaste of future freedom and equality.

      —Nicholas Hesse,
       Western North America

When Henry Wallenkamp left his home in Osnabrück in the 1830s to come to Missouri, he faced a difficult journey. The family group, including more than one hundred persons, first had to travel to a seaport and find a place to stay while they waited for their ship to leave. Sometimes emigrants were forced to wait for weeks while the ship's captain waited for more passengers or favorable weather.

The sea voyage could be difficult or easy, depending on the weather and how many comforts the travelers could afford. Because Wallenkamp's family had more money than many emigrants, they were able to pay for comforts that others could not afford.

Food was a real problem on the long voyages. Until 1855 many ships supplied only water, and passengers had to bring their own food. Nicholas Hesse advised people to take hams, eggs, beer, coffee, lemons, dried fruit, sugar, and other items. Unfortunately, his advice was not practical for the poorer families who could barely afford some of these foods even in normal times.

Even when the ships provided food, the quality was often poor. Sometimes passengers did not get enough to eat. Karl Friedrich Meyer, who emigrated in 1833, recalled that all the

Emigrants wait on the docks in Bremen. Those who traveled to German and other European ports to find ships sailing to America often had long waits before they could leave. (A. E. Schroeder Collection, Western Historical Manuscript Collection–Columbia, courtesy of Countess von Lippe, Institute for Foreign Relations—Stuttgart)

potatoes were gone after only two weeks. He complained that for the remainder of the two-month voyage the diet was mostly "terrible hardtack, sour coffee and tea." Conditions on the voyage were so bad that the passengers almost attacked the captain. He fired his gun into the air to prevent a mutiny.

Henry Wallenkamp had a different complaint about potatoes. He said that the passengers on his voyage never got potatoes to eat, but when the ship reached New Orleans the crew dumped out a large amount of rotten potatoes. He also said that passengers were forced to get by on small amounts of drinking water, but he saw ten large barrels of water poured out in New Orleans.

Ships were very crowded. Only a few wealthy passengers could afford private cabins. It was common for families who could afford cabins to share them with others. Meyer, his wife, and child shared a cabin with a man and his son and daughter.

The man and his children did not speak to the Meyers for the entire voyage.

Most emigrants had to share the large passenger compartments below the deck. These steerage sections were filled to capacity. On a typical ship, people often slept four or six to one bunk. Each adult might have only a seventeen-inch-wide space, with children getting half that. Sometimes ships were so crowded that people had to sleep in hallways or in flimsy shacks on the open decks. Typically there might be one toilet for every fifty passengers, and no tables or chairs for meals.

In these crowded conditions, it was difficult to have any privacy. Hesse commented that passengers quickly got used to being seen in public in their nightgowns. The crowding also quickly turned personal troubles into public scenes. As Meyer reported,

> Every day things happen that make one want to weep or laugh. There is a passenger by the name of Brücking, a strange creature, with his bride. [She] seems to be unfaithful to him, and the little chap took this so to heart that he seemed to have a fit of raving and sat on the deck all afternoon bawling, whereby he aroused the pity of all bystanders.

During pleasant weather passengers could spend most of the time on the ship's deck, but in stormy weather they suffered from the crowded conditions below decks. There the smells of smoke and cooking food mingled with those of seasick passengers and the slop pots used for toilets. People living in port cities said they could always identify immigrant ships by the terrible smell.

The weather also affected how passengers got along with each other. When it was pleasant and the ship was making progress, people were more friendly and tolerant. When they had to be belowdecks for long periods, tempers became short and quarrels were frequent.

Sickness was a serious problem on the ships as well. Typhoid and cholera took a terrible toll on the voyages. In 1854 Congress held an inquiry into sickness on board immigrant ships. Investigators learned that one passenger out of six died or became seriously ill on the voyage. In spite of public concern, illness remained a problem. In the winter of 1867–1868, typhoid fever killed 108 of 544 passengers on a ship from Hamburg.

Funerals at sea were common. There was a case of an eighteen-year-old girl on Meyer's ship, a pleasant and beautiful young woman. She was accompanying her "old deaf and dumb father," who had two other very young children and no wife. When she fell ill, there was nothing that could be done to save her. The passengers pitied the old man who had depended so heavily on her.

Early voyages could take from five weeks to three months, depending on the weather and the speed of the ship. The long voyage was difficult for most of the immigrants, and many lost their lives from illness. For those who survived, however, there was the promise of a better life once they arrived in America.

6

The Journey to Missouri

I [made] a contract with the captain of a boat . . .
to convey our entire company to St. Louis. He was
a fat, good-natured Kentuckian, but his boat was
a shaky old box.
—Friedrich Muench,
Autobiography

Most of the earliest German immigrants landed in eastern
ports such as Philadelphia or Baltimore, but by the 1840s New Orleans had become the most popular destination for those headed
to Missouri. Those who arrived in the East made their way across
the mountains and down the Ohio River to Cincinnati. Many
stayed in Cincinnati, but others continued on the Ohio to the
Mississippi and then upriver to St. Louis.

Friedrich Muench, a leader of an early emigrant society,
reported some unpleasant experiences on his family's journey
from Baltimore to St. Louis in 1834. His group had been at sea
for seven weeks; the overland trip took another four. The group
hired drivers and wagons to carry them across the Allegheny
Mountains to Wheeling, then a part of Virginia. Muench's driver
was no help to him and much trouble. "By nine o'clock in the
morning he was usually drunk, then he lay down in the feedbox
[in the] back of the wagon, fell asleep" and left Muench to drive
the wagon himself. When the drunken driver awoke "he was
usually cross and abusive" so that Muench had to try hard to
avoid getting into fights with the man.

Immigrants to Missouri who arrived in New Orleans had to
find passage on a riverboat. Sometimes the trip up the Mississippi
could be almost as long as the sea voyage. In the early 1800s a
man named Dressler reported that after eight weeks at sea, he
had to spend another six weeks on a riverboat going from New

Orleans to St. Louis. By the 1850s steamboats could make the same trip in less than a week.

Travel on the Mississippi was sometimes even more dangerous than the trip across the Atlantic. Steamboat accidents were common. In 1842 the steamboat *Edna* exploded near the mouth of the Missouri River, killing fifty-five German immigrants. In 1843 the *Big Hatchee* blew up at the wharf in Hermann and killed some seventy people, mostly German immigrants. Thirty-five of those killed are buried on top of the hill at the east end of the City Cemetery, in unmarked graves. Some bodies were never recovered from the river. In 1852 a total of 466 people were killed in sixty-seven steamboat accidents on western rivers. In addition, immigrants were not used to the hot, humid climate along the lower Mississippi; many became ill before they arrived in St. Louis.

Later, travel by train became more common than by riverboat, but conditions did not improve for several decades. The immigrant trains were usually old, crowded, dirty, and short of supplies. It was not until the late 1800s that train travel became more comfortable.

Once the immigrants reached St. Louis, however, they found a small city that was already the "Gateway to the West." The city became the new home of many of the immigrants and the distribution point for those settling elsewhere in Missouri or farther west.

7

Early St. Louis

We live here as in Germany, wholly surrounded
by Germans. Missouri is becoming Germany for
America.
—Emil Mallinckrodt,
Letter, 1847

In its early years, St. Louis was an important distribution
and outfitting center for the nation's rapid westward expansion.
The city's location on the Mississippi River just below the mouth
of the Missouri made it the port of entry for manufactured goods
from the East needed by early settlers. From St. Louis agricultural
products and raw materials were shipped south on steamboats.
Businessmen in St. Louis profited from the nation's westward
growth. The Germans who settled there played an important part
in the economic development of the city.

There were only a few Germans in St. Louis before 1820.
Most of these came from Pennsylvania or other states. One of the
first Germans in St. Louis owned a tavern. Another early German
resident of the city was a teacher. His name was Friedrich Schewe,
and he sold candles on the side to supplement his teaching
income.

Years later, when Friedrich Steines arrived in St. Louis in
the summer of 1834, there were about eighteen German families
and a few unmarried Germans among the city's seven thousand
residents. That summer the flood of German immigration to
Missouri began.

Steines is an example of the German immigrants who came
to St. Louis in the 1830s. He was a teacher from Prussia who
led the Solingen Emigration Society to Missouri to find freedom from government harassment. They arrived in July, and
before the end of the month his wife and four children died of

This lithograph by Eduard Robyn shows St. Louis as it looked from the Illinois side of the Mississippi in the mid-1800s. Three Robyn brothers emigrated to Missouri from Emmerich, a German town near the Dutch border, in the 1830s and 1840s. (State Historical Society of Missouri, Columbia)

cholera. The Solingen Society broke up, and Steines moved to Franklin County, where he started a school for boys. For many years St. Louis German families sent their sons to his Oakfield Academy to study mathematics, the sciences, and languages.

In spite of reports of harsh winters and outbreaks of terrible diseases like the one that devastated the Steines family, German immigrants continued to pour into St. Louis, believing that life would be better for them in America.

In 1835 the *Missouri Republican* reported, "Every steamboat that arrives at our wharves is crowded with passengers." Five years later the same newspaper commented: "One might imagine that 'the world and his family' are coming here. We have never witnessed such crowds of people as throng our streets. . . . The hotels, boarding houses, etc. are crowded to excess."

The new settlers and immigrants included many Germans. In the 1840s Emil Mallinckrodt wrote to his brother, "One often imagines he is in Germany when he hears low German and the patter of wooden shoes clattering in the streets . . . All Germans are without exception well off. They own one-third of St. Louis."

The Germans in St. Louis owned saloons, restaurants, grocery stores, and boardinghouses. They were carpenters and furniture makers, blacksmiths, barbers, doctors, and druggists. The thousands of Germans who made St. Louis their home in the 1830s, 1840s, and 1850s brought skills that were desperately needed in the rapidly growing city. The city needed shoemakers, tailors, bakers, brewers, and other skilled workmen. With the numbers of people pouring into the city each year, housing was always in short supply and carpenters, stone masons, bricklayers, and painters were especially in demand. Those without skills could usually find work as cooks, maids, nurses, gardeners, or day laborers.

Temporary lodging was the most pressing need for the new immigrants. Many found lodging in one of the hotels or boardinghouses on the riverfront. The city's life centered on the river, and small, crowded settlements developed along its banks.

Because of the overcrowded conditions, St. Louis became one of the unhealthiest cities in the world. Many people died from diseases. The city also suffered from disasters. There was a devastating flood in the spring of 1844. A huge fire that started on the waterfront in 1849 destroyed fifteen square blocks of the city. That same year a cholera epidemic killed almost a tenth of the people who lived in St. Louis.

In spite of these problems, the city continued to grow and prosper. By 1850 St. Louis had grown to nearly seventy-eight thousand people, including nearly twenty-four thousand Germans. German newspapers, social clubs, theaters, and musical groups thrived there.

8

Latin Farmers and Settlement Societies

They had wielded the pen, but had never handled the hoe; they had stood in the pulpit but never behind a plow.
 —E. D. Kargau,
  Missouri's German Immigration

I soon learned to handle the native axe, learned to plow, to sow, to mow.
 —Friedrich Muench

Some of the first Germans to settle west of St. Louis located near Gottfried Duden's farm in Warren County. They were members of emigration societies, groups formed to establish settlements in the New World that promised freedom and opportunity.

The settlements that grew up in eastern Missouri contained many German university graduates who were able to read Latin but were not used to farmwork. They came to be called "Latin Farmers."

Some people believe that the Germans were able to succeed because they were able to select the best land. However, one contemporary commented that, among the Latin Farmers, those who got good land deserved no praise and those who got poor land deserved no criticism: "Not one of them was a competent judge of land."

The members of the Berlin Society established Dutzow in Warren County in the 1830s. Most of them were wealthy professional men and some were even minor nobility. Johann Wilhelm Bock, a leader of the group who was called "Baron von Bock," had been a wealthy landowner in Germany. Bock named Dutzow after his estate in Mecklenburg. He named the streets of the town for German poets and built a club for friends and neighbors.

The Bock family was famous among German travelers for their parties. They had the only piano within miles. They and others in the group had come to live an idealized life on the farm without understanding how much hard work was required.

Some of the dreams of these wealthier immigrants were idealistic and impractical. One of Bock's schemes was to make Lake Creek, which ran through his property, large enough for steamboats. The problem, according to a neighbor of his, was that the creek was so small it could "be crossed dry footed in many places." Bock, however, proposed to dig a canal four miles long to the Missouri River so that boats could bring rich Southern planters to spend summers at a fashionable hotel he would build in Dutzow.

The Giessener Society was another group formed in Germany that brought Germans to Missouri. Led by Friedrich Muench and his friend and brother-in-law Paul Follenius, the society developed plans to concentrate Germans in a territory that could eventually be admitted to the Union as a German state. The group's five hundred members included writers, clergymen, and lawyers, but many had little experience with a plow or an axe.

They came in two groups. The first group, led by Follenius through New Orleans, held the Society's money. When Muench arrived in St. Louis with the second group of sixty families, he found his friend ill, the first group scattered, and the money gone. Muench and Follenius used their own funds to pay the members of the second group for what they had lost. The two eventually settled with only a handful of families near the site of Duden's farm. Muench wrote many articles for German and German-American newspapers as "Far West." He was somewhat critical of his neighbor Bock, who had built a clubhouse before he built his home.

After an economic depression in 1837 ruined many of the Latin Farmers financially, several committed suicide and others returned to Germany. Many who stayed were the poorer immigrants who had been hired by the Latin Farmers to do farmwork. Some of the immigrants from wealthy families also stayed and

Paul Follenius was a lawyer from Giessen who used the Latin form of his name rather than its original German form, Follen. According to his friend Friedrich Muench, "He learned to swing an axe as well as any man." Follenius died of typhoid in 1844, only ten years after arriving in Missouri. (State Historical Society of Missouri, Columbia)

supported themselves with their labor. For example, one became a tanner and another took a job as a land surveyor.

The grand schemes of these groups often failed. Bock's canal was never dug, and Dutzow never became a summer resort for wealthy planters. The emigration societies were unable to create a New Germany as a separate state. They were not even successful in bringing large numbers of people to Missouri. Only a scattering of people from the areas where the societies recruited ever came to Missouri. Most immigrants came alone or in family groups.

Some of those who came with the societies became important in Missouri history, however. They contributed to the political and economic development of the state. Friedrich Muench, for example, served in the Missouri legislature and was a leader in developing the early wine industry in Missouri.

9

Missouri's Little Germany

The German School of Hermann . . . [shall] forever remain a German school.
—Missouri General Assembly Charter, 1848

The Germans who founded Hermann had a grand vision of a city where German culture could flourish in the New World. The German Settlement Society of Philadelphia was formed in 1836 to build a colony where German language, values, and traditions could be maintained.

The Settlement Society sent a scouting committee to visit Illinois, Indiana, Missouri, Michigan, and Wisconsin to look for a location for the colony. The scouts were told to look for land that was near a river and would be good for growing grain and fruit and for raising sheep and cattle.

The scouting committee recommended a site in Missouri on the Gasconade River. They may have been influenced by the fact that there were already Germans living in this area. They may also have liked this land because it reminded them of the river valleys in Germany.

The Society sent George F. Bayer, a teacher, to buy the land. Because the area the scouts had recommended was not available, he bought 11,300 acres of land a little to the east, in the hilly area along the Missouri River. Founders in Philadelphia named the colony "Hermann" in honor of the Germanic hero who had defeated the Romans in the year 9 A.D.

The Settlement Society believed Hermann would become a rival to St. Louis. They made grand plans for the city, mapping out public squares and naming streets for famous Germans and Americans. Many of their plans were impossible to carry out because the land was so hilly. However, there are streets in Hermann today named for Gutenberg, Schiller, Mozart, Washington, Jefferson, and other famous men.

Seventeen people, including eight children, arrived at the settlement in December 1837 on the last steamboat of the season. Bayer was on his way to Hermann at the time, but he became ill and was delayed many weeks in Pittsburgh. His delay in arriving caused problems because he was the only person with the authority to lay out and assign lots to people. Winter was setting in, and the colonists were desperate to start building their homes.

The early settlers had a hard time that first winter. They survived with the help of the Hensley family and the widow Polly Phillips, who lived in one-room cabins on Frene Creek.

Another group of colony members planned better. Instead of showing up in the wilderness in the middle of winter, they came as far as St. Louis, looked for temporary work, and waited for Bayer. They moved to Hermann in the spring of 1838.

Developing their town was more difficult than the organizers expected, in part because they asked too much from Bayer. He was to survey all the land, assign property to the colonists, furnish food for all the settlers, arrange for sawmills and gristmills to be built, and deal with complaints. And the settlers had many complaints. In fact, they complained so much that the Society lost confidence in Bayer and released him from his duties. His health had suffered under the demands placed on him, and Bayer died in March 1839 at the age of thirty-nine.

Not long after they arrived, some of the settlers began to call for self-government and for a separation from the Society in Philadelphia. By December 1839 the Settlement Society had transferred its property to a board of trustees in Hermann.

The town grew in spite of the problems. A year after the first settlers arrived, Hermann had five stores, two large hotels, and a post office. A brass band had been formed, and there were two shooting clubs, each with about fifty members.

Some of the settlers were unhappy because very little of the land Bayer had bought was good for farming. However, it turned out to be excellent for vineyards. The vineyards contributed to Hermann's economic success, along with the production of beer, whiskey, and shoes. The town became an important shipping

Stone Hill Winery in Hermann became one of the largest wineries in the world. These original buildings remain in use today. Vineyards were planted on many of the hillsides around the town. (State Historical Society of Missouri, Columbia)

point on the Missouri River. In the heyday of the steamboat era, Hermann was the busiest port on the river. Charles Eitzen, who owned a general store in Hermann, added to his fortune by hauling iron ore from the Maramec Iron Furnaces and pine lumber from Ozarks forests to be shipped by steamboat and rail from Hermann.

Town leaders built a market house in 1856. The lower floor had stalls for sellers of meat, eggs, dairy products, vegetables, and other products. The second story was one large hall that served as a city hall and a public meeting room.

Education was always important in Hermann, because it was a way to preserve German culture. By the fall of 1839, the first school building was ready, and a teacher had been hired. He was paid $250 for the year and given a $50 lot in town. The students went to school in the mornings during the summer, and for five hours a day during the winter, with no school on Wednesday and Saturday afternoons. They studied German, English, arithmetic, history, geography, and drawing.

The trustees often visited the school to check on the progress of the children. After a school district was formed in 1842, the town donated land to it. Later the town sold land to benefit a town-school fund. In 1848 the Missouri legislature passed a law that provided that the school in Hermann should "forever remain a German school." The law allowed courses to be taught in German in all grades. This practice continued for more than seventy-five years.

Hermann never became a city to rival St. Louis, but it did become a strong center of German culture. It came to be known throughout the state as "Little Germany." Its residents enjoyed a life that was rich in German tradition with wineries and German newspapers, theater, and music. Its festivities attracted many visitors and continue to do so to this day.

10

Log Cabins and Corn Bread

> The first two years are the most difficult because of the change in climate, the hardships of domestic life, and homesickness, all of which can afflict the healthiest body and endanger people's lives.
> —Gottfried Duden,
> *Report on a Journey to the Western States of North America*

The first German settlers on the Missouri frontier faced many hardships. Henriette Bruns, called Jette, arrived in Westphalia with her husband, Dr. Bernhard Bruns, in 1836. They were accompanied by their young son, Jette's two brothers, a maid, and a workman. This group of seven moved into a log cabin that was no larger than the living room of Jette's home in Germany.

Unlike Bruns, many of the new immigrants were peasant farmers who arrived with no money. The long journey from Europe had taken everything they had. A priest who worked with the Germans in Osage County commented that often they survived because of the charity of their American neighbors. "I have heard several German families saying that when they came . . . they were in great poverty and obliged to beg. . . . The Americans were good; they never grew tired of our asking, but simply said 'take it.'"

The newcomers borrowed tools, cut trees, and built log cabins with temporary roofs made of cornstalks and leaves. They made do with what they had. Before mills were built, the settlers used coffee mills brought from Europe for grinding corn. They made wagons entirely of wood, fastened with wooden bolts, with rounds sawed from the trunks of sycamore trees for wheels.

Unlike the Latin Farmers, the German peasants knew what kind of land they wanted. They quickly selected the best of

31

Building a log cabin was often a community project. American neighbors taught the new German immigrants skills they needed on the Missouri frontier. (State Historical Society of Missouri, Columbia)

Jette Bruns's 1850 sketch (redrawn by Frank Stack) of the house she and Dr. Bruns built in Westphalia. It was quite lavish compared to their first home, a simple log cabin with one window. (Geisberg-Bruns Collection, courtesy of A. E. Schroeder)

the land available and gradually bought out their American neighbors in many areas. Russel Gerlach, a geographer, says that a map of the best soils in Missouri would be almost identical to a map of the German settlements.

Even for those who were experienced at farming, the work was hard. They faced long days clearing land, planting crops, and building cabins, barns, and fences. The Americans taught them to split logs into rails and build rail fences.

Some of the crops grown in America, such as corn, were new to the Germans. They had to learn how to grow and use these crops from their American neighbors. German women were used to baking bread with rye or wheat flour, but they quickly learned to bake corn bread, something completely new to them.

Successes were mixed with setbacks. Gert Goebel reports that in 1839 a plague of squirrels destroyed much of the corn crop in many of the German settlements along the Missouri. The

William Pelster from Dissen in the province of Westphalia began building this house barn to shelter his family and his farm animals in Franklin County in 1855. The four-story building included living quarters for the family, cattle stalls, a threshing floor, and a hayloft. Very few house barns were built in the United States. (Nick Decker, Missouri Department of Natural Resources)

squirrels came from the north and were so numerous that they swam the river to get to the crops on the southern side. The price of corn meal more than doubled that winter. In 1841 a drought ruined crops and brought many settlers to the brink of starvation. The Bruns family had fences washed away in spring floods, potatoes ruined by drought, and baby pigs frozen in winter.

The Germans were used to having neighbors and family close by. On the frontier they were often miles from their nearest neighbors and half a world away from their families in Germany. Loneliness and homesickness were problems for many.

In addition to other hardships, diseases like typhoid fever, cholera, and influenza were serious dangers. Cholera was particularly dangerous. In 1849 the riverboat *Monroe* landed at Jefferson City with two passengers dead of cholera and several others ill.

All but two of the boat's officers deserted in fear. In four days thirty-seven passengers died, and another fifteen died in the next week. Towns could be devastated by a cholera outbreak.

Often the immigrants came to Missouri with dreams of giving their children a better life than was possible in Germany. Sometimes, however, those children were taken from them by illness. Five years after they settled in Westphalia, the Bruns family became ill with dysentery. They lost three of their four children within three weeks. The cemeteries of the German towns contain many children's graves, reminders of the losses of families who had left home for their children's sake.

Those who survived usually saw their lives improve. As more Germans moved in, farms became less isolated. In Osage County, for example, German settlement began in 1835. By 1850 the county's population was sixty-seven hundred. Ten years later no family in Westphalia was headed by a native-born American. As the population grew, popular social activities became possible. Singing societies, shooting clubs, and other social groups made life more enjoyable.

Economic conditions eventually improved for the early settlers. The life of Henry Wallenkamp provides an example of how many German immigrants improved their economic situations. In 1840 the Wallenkamp family settled near Washington, Missouri, where neighbors from Osnabrück already lived.

Henry was sent to school in St. Louis. He returned to Washington in 1843 and opened a store in a two-story log cabin near town. Although it was a small town, his store was the fourth in the area. Nevertheless, he became successful and soon moved into a building in Washington.

Transporting freight was a problem for merchants like Wallenkamp. Farmers who were making a trip to St. Louis took his eggs, butter, and bacon to the city and returned with goods he needed in the store.

When Wallenkamp needed to travel to the city, he tried paying for a ride on one of the farm wagons. The ride cost fifty cents each way, and passengers had to agree to walk up hills to rest the horses. He decided that he could walk the entire way and save a dollar. He started early in the morning, carrying his noon meal with him, and walked to the city. There he paid twenty-five cents for supper, lodging, and the next morning's breakfast. After breakfast he took care of his business and walked home.

His business grew as the farms in the area prospered. In addition to operating his store, he provided services such as shipping farmers' crops to St. Louis. Many boatloads of tobacco, for example, left Washington for St. Louis. Because of his education, he was able to write deeds and contracts for his neighbors. Only two people in Washington could read and write English well enough to do this work.

The willingness to work at whatever jobs were available was typical of the successful immigrants. Through their ability to learn new skills and work hard, they saw their lives improve. Often their dreams of better lives for their children did come true.

11

Frontier Women

> How lonely I am here—no woman who thinks as
> I do, with whom now and then I could exchange
> my feelings when I need that kind of relief, when
> I want to forget the daily troubles and sorrows,
> when they could be set aside for a short time.
> —Jette Geisberg Bruns,
> Letter, June 14, 1840

Jette Bruns was the daughter of the mayor in the Westphalian city of Oelde. Her mother died when she was thirteen, and she took care of her brothers and sisters. She was very close to her family and was happy with her life in Oelde. However, her husband, Dr. Bernhard Bruns, caught the emigration fever that was sweeping through the German provinces. He became convinced he could provide a better life for his family in America.

In 1836 Jette reluctantly left her home, family, and friends to accompany her husband to a new Westphalia, a lonely settlement in frontier Missouri. She was twenty-three.

Jette was determined to do her best to make the move successful. In the early years she wrote many cheerful letters to her brother Heinrich and other relatives. In 1840 Jette described their flourishing crops and gardens in a letter to Heinrich:

> On our farm the wheat and rye are flourishing. . . . the corn, potatoes, etc. are doing well. . . . This year all the plants are just as abundant as they used to be in Germany; the beautiful flowers delight the boys.

Disaster struck the next year when the family fell ill with dysentery and three of the four children died within three weeks. Over the years, Jette lost five young children and a son who

37

Jette Bruns is shown here with three of her children. The family moved to Jefferson City in the 1850s. After the death of her husband during the Civil War, Jette ran a boardinghouse across the street from the capitol building to support her family. It was called "The German Diet" because so many German legislators stayed there. (Geisberg-Bruns Collection, courtesy of A. E. Schroeder)

was killed in the Civil War. Later in her life Jette wrote, "I have reproached myself bitterly that I did not object more strongly to a move to a country to which I had little attraction and which robbed me for life of many pleasures."

Life on the farms could be hard, even without illness. German women often worked in the fields with their husbands and children. A woman's day on a frontier farm involved hard work and long hours.

John Buse grew up on a farm near St. Charles in the 1860s and 1870s. He described his mother's workday during the busy harvest season this way. When the hay was ready to cut, the men started working in the fields as soon as it was daylight. His mother had to get up early enough to milk the cows, feed the chickens, and have breakfast ready at four o'clock. After breakfast she would do her housework and then go out to help in the fields.

She took her baby with her, putting her down in the shade of a stack of wheat. She would help pitch hay while her husband stacked it. She would stop at times to nurse the baby and then return to her work.

Around nine o'clock, she would go home, make the morning lunch, and bring it to the field. Around eleven, she would collect the empty lunch dishes and go home to prepare the main meal of the day. The men took two hours for dinner, mostly to rest the horses, but she got no rest. By the time she looked after the baby, washed the dishes, and prepared the afternoon meal, it was time to go back to the field. She worked in the field until dark, and then went home to prepare supper. While she was fixing supper, the men fed and watered the animals and made sure the farm equipment was ready for use the next day. They went to bed after supper, but her work was still not done. She had to wash dishes again, get things ready for breakfast, and attend to the baby's needs. Then she could go to bed. The next day would come early.

A farm wife's load was a little lighter at other times of the year, but frontier life was filled with long days in every season. More prosperous settlers hired both men and women as live-in laborers on farms, and this helped. Older children were expected to work. Even younger children helped out. Often they were the ones who tended the chickens and carried the lunches to the workers in the fields.

Homesickness was a common problem, especially for women. Many frontier women who lived on isolated farms suffered from loneliness and depression. For immigrant women who could not speak English and who were far from their families in Germany, conditions were sometimes more than they could bear.

Like Nicholas Hesse's wife, many suffered from a devastating homesickness. Jette Bruns's first visit to the Hesses upset her badly because Mrs. Hesse cried and complained that she couldn't stand it there. Jette believed the Hesses returned to Europe because of Mrs. Hesse's unhappiness. She was determined to stay, but homesickness sometimes overcame her, too.

Jette understood how difficult life on the frontier could be for women. After the Hesses left, she wrote to her brother: "A great deal of patience and perseverance are necessary in the beginning; otherwise I am afraid that Mrs. Hesse will find all kinds of women who will follow her back."

Women in towns such as Washington and Augusta had more opportunities to improve the quality of their lives than did women on isolated farms. The frequent concerts, plays, community dinners, and informal evening gatherings must have helped overcome the sadness of separation from family and friends in Germany.

Friedrich Muench's son, Hugo, remarked that the women who emigrated deserved much of the credit for any success the Germans had. Unfortunately, almost everything we know of the lives, hardships, and dreams of these women depends on what we are told by the men who knew them.

The early German housewife was often described as strong, hardworking, clean, and quiet. She put aside her own desires for the good of her husband and family. Friedrich Muench described good German housewives who had followed their husbands to America:

They are . . . never plagued by boredom, and find their satisfaction in the work they do every day for the welfare of their families. They keep the house clean and in order, do all the cooking,

This photograph by Edward Kemper shows a group of workers in his vineyard near Hermann. German farm women often worked alongside men in the fields. (Kemper Collection, Western Historical Manuscript Collection–Columbia, courtesy of Anna Hesse)

> baking, washing, knitting, mending, sewing, . . . care for the children, milk the cows, make butter and cheese, dry fruit, make jam, can fruits and vegetables, make soap, take care of the flower and vegetable garden, tend to the fowls, and some even weave the most necessary cloth for the household; and in spite of all this they do not cease to live as people of culture.

Muench's comments reflect the attitudes of the middle class. Not all of the farm women were able "to live as people of culture." They were sometimes criticized by middle-class men for not behaving properly. For example, some men were offended when they saw a woman riding astride a horse rather than sidesaddle as a lady should.

Women's work in the home, whether in cities and towns or on frontier farms, was important to the family's economic

Luise Fritz Muench was a source of inspiration for both her husband and her son, Hugo. They wrote of her life as a pioneer woman, but unfortunately her own thoughts about the life of the German housewife in Missouri were not recorded. Her eighteen-year-old son was killed in the Civil War battle at Wilson's Creek. (State Historical Society of Missouri, Columbia)

success. In addition, women's skills helped preserve food traditions and folk customs that were important in retaining the
family's cultural identity for so long. Their support of church,
school, and social activities was also important in preserving
German cultural life and the use of the German language.

12

Religious Life in Osage County

In western Osage County, the Catholic Church, dominated by Germans, remains supreme to this day.
—Russel Gerlach,
Immigrants in the Ozarks

The churches of Westphalia, Loose Creek, Rich Fountain, Frankenstein, and other Osage County communities show the vitality of the religious culture of the area. Like the churches of their German homeland, the churches of these settlements were built on hills, and their steeples can be seen from miles around, rising above the houses. They are both the physical and the cultural centers of their communities.

Many of the earliest settlers in Osage County were Roman Catholic. Before the bishop in St. Louis assigned a priest to Osage County, the settlers said their prayers and worshipped in less formal ways. For example, children in the settlement gathered flowers and placed them around a statue of the Virgin Mary to honor her. The settlers in Westphalia built a small chapel on a hill adjoining their farms in 1837.

Church authorities in St. Louis wanted to encourage more Catholics to settle in central Missouri. The bishop sent Father Ferdinand Helias, a Belgian missionary, to Westphalia to serve as pastor in May 1838. A year later a settler wrote, "Church and school are now active, and there are already seven craftsmen living on the church land. . . . A large Catholic settlement of 400 people has been formed."

Father Helias had joined the Jesuit order to serve the Indians, but he spent his life among the German immigrants in central

Missouri. He and other Jesuit priests helped establish more than thirty churches in the area.

The lives of these pioneer missionaries were not easy. They traveled from one village to another on horseback, often before roads were built. When they traveled, they stayed in the cabins of families who had to fit them into already crowded rooms.

Father Helias had problems getting along with some of the residents of Westphalia. Some objected to the strong opinions of the Jesuits. One visitor to the community complained that the parishioners were instructed to subscribe to a Catholic newspaper and were forbidden to read other papers.

Helias got into a dispute with Dr. Bernhard Bruns that ended in a court suit. Helias won the case, but it divided the community. Bruns also complained to Helias's superiors that he was interfering in politics. These problems frustrated Helias so much that he finally left the Westphalia parish, posting a notice in Latin on the church door:

> Why should one looking for trouble go to the Indians, let him come to Westphalia.
> There he will find trouble enough.

He devoted the remaining thirty years of his life to his mixed German and Belgian congregation at Taos and other communities in central and western Missouri. He was the chaplain at the Missouri State Penitentiary, and traveled as far west as Benton County.

In spite of these difficulties, the churches became the centers of community life. Schools were founded, even in rural communities. There were elementary schools where German was the language of instruction along with English. Convents were built to house the nuns who came to teach. Sometimes rural children stayed in the convents during the winter months. Many of the young women from the villages looked to these women as models and entered religious orders to become teaching or nursing nuns.

The Germans of Osage County had less contact with the outside world than those in most of the other settlements in the Missouri River Valley. There was no thriving river port nearby, and the residents had limited contact with St. Louis and other

Anna Gertrude Kleinsorge, who became Sister Mary Heribertha, was a member of the School Sisters of Notre Dame in 1875. She grew up in Westphalia and was one of many young women from Catholic towns who found careers in religious orders that provided teachers and nurses. (A. E. Schroeder Collection, Western Historical Manuscript Collection–Columbia, courtesy of Ed Bode)

Schoolchildren and adults in Westphalia in the early summer of 1890 celebrate the religious feast of *Corpus Christi*. The feast day was marked by decorations and parades including religious services in the streets of many German communities. (Missouri State Archives, courtesy of Westphalia Historical Society)

commercial centers. Long after the Civil War, the county still exported products typical of a frontier economy: game, tallow, hides, fur, and lumber. Because of their isolation, the communities of Osage County maintained their German language and customs well into the first half of this century. The use of German in church services for so long contributed to the preservation of the language.

Whether they were Catholic or Protestant, churches were important in the German communities. The major Protestant groups were Lutherans, Methodists, and German Evangelicals. Religion played an important role in the lives of many of the German immigrants, and it continues to do so for their descendants today.

Church buildings still dominate the horizon in many towns, adding beauty to the Missouri landscape. The churches established in the early days continue to thrive. The German churches and schools frequently form the center of the communities. While many small towns in the state have lost both population and most of their small businesses, the German towns have suffered less as a result of this than others. Their churches have bonded the communities together, helping them to maintain their identity.

13

The Cradle of the Lutheran Church in America

> The German church here, almost more than anything else, assures the continued use of the German language and preserves the national characteristics.
>
> —Friedrich Muench,
> *State of Missouri*

In 1837 Martin Stephan, a Lutheran minister in the Kingdom of Saxony, found himself in trouble with the police and officials of the Lutheran Church. He was suspended from his position as pastor of St. John's Church in the city of Dresden. Stephan had been the pastor at St. John's for twenty-eight years, and he had a large number of loyal supporters in his congregation.

Martin Stephan formed an emigration society, and several hundred of his followers decided to go with him to build a new religious community in Missouri. They pooled their money into a common fund to pay for the group's journey to St. Louis and to purchase land for their settlement. Stephan's son Martin decided to go with him, but his wife, Julie, and seven daughters chose to stay in Dresden.

Over the course of several days in November 1838, 665 people left the port of Bremen in five ships. The last two ships, the *Olbers* and the *Amalia*, set sail on Sunday, November 18. Not long after it reached the Atlantic Ocean, the *Olbers* was hit by a severe storm that terrified Stephan and the other passengers. The captain ordered the portholes nailed shut and the lamps extinguished. The *Amalia* probably sank during the storm because it never arrived in New Orleans. Stephan's followers who were on the ship, forty-three adults and fifteen children, died when it was lost at sea.

The Saxon Lutherans needed temporary lodging in St. Louis while a site could be chosen for their new community. At that time the population of the city was about sixteen thousand, so it was a difficult task to find housing for a group of some six hundred new immigrants.

Many of Stephan's followers were miserable in St. Louis. Prices were high, and they had a hard time getting enough to eat. The city was crowded and unhealthy. Many of the Saxon immigrants became ill, and nearly seventy of them died.

Meanwhile, Stephan lived extravagantly, eating fine food in his well-furnished and carpeted rooms. He spent the group's money freely on an expensive carriage, a library, an organ and other musical instruments, a bishop's cross on a chain of pure gold, and fine wines. After a few months in St. Louis, nearly all the money was gone.

Using virtually the last of their money, the Saxon Lutherans bought about forty-five hundred acres of land along the Mississippi River in Perry County. In April 1839 the first colonists left St. Louis for the settlement.

Less than two weeks later, Stephan was disgraced when several women confessed to having sexual relations with him. He was charged with adultery, misuse of the funds of others, rejecting the word of God, and other offenses. The pastors and laymen voted to remove him from office.

Stephan was given the choice of returning to Germany, facing trial, or being transported across the river to Illinois. He chose Illinois.

A council of church leaders gave Stephan one hundred dollars and allowed him to keep his Bible, some clothes, and a few household items. They arranged for him to rent a room on a farm on the Illinois side of the river. Two members of the group rowed Stephan across the Mississippi River and set him ashore with a spade and an axe.

Stephan never admitted to any of the charges against him, but his maid, Louise Guenther, confessed that she had been his mistress for several years. Two weeks after his removal, she left the colony and joined Stephan in Illinois. She stayed with him until he died in 1846.

After Stephan's departure, many of the immigrants decided to stay in St. Louis, where they had better job opportunities. Some

The Log Cabin College, located in Altenburg, had an ambitious course of study. The college remained open only until 1843. Later the Missouri Synod founded Concordia Seminary in St. Louis. (State Historical Society of Missouri, Columbia)

members of the group returned to Germany. Many of Stephan's followers who were still in Saxony decided to stay there, although a group of 141 people joined the earlier immigrants late in 1839. Most of the Saxons who came to Missouri with Stephan eventually settled into a new life in southeastern Perry County. Several towns were established there, including Wittenberg, Altenburg, Frohna, Johannisberg, and Paitzdorf, which was renamed Uniontown after the Civil War.

The weather was good the first summer the settlers were in Perry County, and their American neighbors had good harvests. They donated loads of apples and sacks of flour to their new German neighbors. Often the Germans repaid them by knitting and sewing for them.

In their first years in the wilderness, the colonists suffered from malaria, extreme poverty, and the harsh demands of pioneer work. In spite of the help they received from the Americans, a large number of the Germans died.

The Saxon communities in Perry County survived the first difficult early years under the leadership of Pastor C. F. W.

Trinity Evangelical Lutheran Church in St. Louis, affectionately called "Old Trinity," is the mother church of the Lutheran congregations in the area. It was founded by some of the Saxon Lutherans who never left the city to join their companions in Perry County. (State Historical Society of Missouri, Columbia)

Walther. In spite of their poverty, the group's leaders made plans to open a college. The log cabin school, opened in December 1839, offered courses in six languages, religion, geography, history, mathematics, science, philosophy, music, and drawing. Both young men and young women attended the Log Cabin Seminary.

The Evangelical Lutheran Synod of Missouri, Ohio, and Other States was founded in 1847. C. F. W. Walther was its first president. In this century the church was renamed the Lutheran Church—Missouri Synod, reflecting its birth in Missouri. Today the Missouri Synod is the largest association of Lutheran churches in the United States.

14

Bread, Water, and Hard Work

A republic of workers, living in equality, desiring
peace and renouncing riches.
—Johann Valentin Andreae,
Christopolis, 1619

Wilhelm Keil and his wife Luise left the Kingdom of Prussia in the 1830s to come to America. Keil worked briefly as a tailor in New York before the couple settled in Pittsburgh and opened a drugstore.

In Pittsburgh Keil sold drugs and gave out medical advice. People called him "Dr. Keil." His reputation grew because he had a bottle of a mysterious medicine and a book of secret cures for various illnesses. The book was filled with strange symbols written in blood. It had been given to Keil by an old woman in Germany who was known for her skill in healing the sick. Some people called Keil the *"Hexendoktor,"* or "witch doctor."

In 1838 Keil was converted at a German Methodist revival meeting. In a dramatic ceremony witnessed by the Methodist preacher, he burned his mysterious book of cures and put his days as a witch doctor behind him. He was soon licensed as a preacher.

After a few troubled years with different Methodist churches, Keil rejected all organized churches to become an independent preacher. He was young and a powerful public speaker. Soon he had a large following, and his teachings spread throughout western Pennsylvania, southern Ohio, Virginia, Indiana, Kentucky, and Iowa.

Keil decided to form a community based on the teachings of the Bible. He promised his followers nothing but bread, water,

The town of Bethel was different from other German settlements in Missouri. It was a Christian communal society in which people shared both their labor and the fruits of their labor, hoping to form a perfect community on earth. (State Historical Society of Missouri, Columbia)

and hard work, but many sold their property and pooled their money into a common fund. In the spring of 1844, Keil sent three men to find land for a permanent colony. They bought more than twenty-five hundred acres in the valley of the North River in Shelby County, Missouri.

Keil and the first settlers arrived in the fall of 1844. The colony was named Bethel, after an ancient city near Jerusalem. The word "Bethel" means "the house of God" in Hebrew. Within a few years more than six hundred people lived in Bethel.

Keil's followers were looking for the perfect society, based on the idea of communal living. Each family was given a house. Food was distributed on Saturday each week, and clothing was provided in the spring and fall. People worked where they were able and where they were most needed. There was a common field for growing corn, grains, and other crops. Herds of cattle and sheep grazed on the prairies. A huge barn was built for the workhorses.

A Bethel resident named Beatrice Finck described her daily work in a letter to her relatives in Germany. "Besides attending to

Education was important in Bethel, as in other German communities. The brick school shown here was built near the church. (State Historical Society of Missouri, Columbia)

the things my dear mother taught me, such as cooking, baking, washing, ironing, sewing, knitting, mending, etc . . . Well, I can milk a cow, which gives me great pleasure; also I can make trousers, vests, and coats. There is no work I dodge and I am not ashamed to perform the humblest tasks; . . . I often sing from morn to night."

A mile east of town the colonists built a large brick home for Keil and his family. It had a ballroom on the second floor that was used for community gatherings and space on the third floor for Keil's botanical laboratory.

The church building was the showcase of the colony. When it was built, it was the largest church west of the Mississippi River. It was built of brick and stone and had a tower almost eighty feet tall. Inside, the church had a red tile floor and was finished with the beautiful wood of the black walnut trees in the area. The bricks and most of the other materials for the church were made in the colony. Only the windows, nails, and bells had to be purchased. The church had two doors, one for men and one for women. During services men sat on one side of the building and women sat on the other.

This store on the main street of Bethel still stands today. (State Historical Society of Missouri, Columbia)

Christmas in the Bethel colony was a grand affair. The Christmas service included a band concert, a sermon, and singing. Many visitors from outside the colony came for the celebration. Baskets of cakes, apples, and candy were shared among all.

In 1855 Keil and many of his followers left Bethel to start a new colony in the Northwest. They made the trip in a seventy-five-wagon train. A six-mule wagon carrying the coffin of Keil's oldest son, William, led the train. He had been promised before his death that he would be able to go west with the others. William was buried when the group reached Washington Territory.

Until his death in 1877, Keil continued to govern the colony at Bethel by letter from Oregon, but the communal society was dissolved after he died. The property owned by the colony was divided among the residents. Most of the families in Bethel stayed in their homes, making their living from farming or in trades. Many years later one of the colonists recalled, "We were not wealthy, but we had all that we needed and were happy."

Today more than thirty of the sturdy buildings from the colony days remain, and Bethel residents sponsor festivals and other events to attract visitors to the town.

15

Among the Americans

The Germans [in Boonville] . . . gain wealth, have
a music society, a singing society, a Turner society,
and live on friendly footing with the Americans.
　　　—Friedrich Muench,
　　　State of Missouri

Many of the immigrants who came from Germany did not
settle in towns that were predominantly German. Along the Missouri River west of Osage County and in other parts of the state,
Germans were almost always a minority wherever they made
their homes. In his 1859 survey of the "most important cities" in
Missouri, Friedrich Muench listed those with significant German
populations. These included New Madrid, Cape Girardeau, and
Ste. Genevieve in southeast Missouri, Hannibal in the northeast,
and Springfield and Warsaw toward the west.

As the population of the state expanded to the west, the
Missouri legislature decided to move the capital from St. Charles
to Jefferson City. The new state capitol building was completed in
1840 by German immigrant stonemasons. Many Germans came
to Jefferson City in the 1840s and 1850s. A Prussian immigrant
named Charles Lohman bought the store at the steamboat landing in 1852. In 1855 his partner Charles Maus built a large brick
hotel next to their store. It was renamed the Union Hotel after
Maus served as a captain in the Union army during the Civil
War. Gerhardt Dulle, another early German immigrant, built a
small grain mill just west of the capitol building in the mid-1850s.
The mill prospered and became one of Jefferson City's largest
industries. Although the businesses are long gone, Jefferson City
residents still refer to these areas as "Lohman's Landing" and the
"mill bottom."

The new state capitol was built high on a bluff overlooking the Missouri River. Charles Lohman's store at left was conveniently close to the riverboat landing. (State Historical Society of Missouri, Columbia)

Farther west along the Missouri River, Germans became members of mostly English-speaking communities in Boonville, Arrow Rock, Glasgow, Brunswick, Lexington, and other towns. Small groups of Germans developed notable German communities, including Cole Camp and Concordia, as well as other towns in Pettis, Benton, Saline, Lafayette, and Johnson Counties. The other early settlers in these counties were mainly Americans from the eastern United States.

The Germans also formed sizable minorities in the larger cities of Kansas City and St. Joseph. A Prussian immigrant named Frederick W. Smith moved to the Blacksnake Hills in Platte County in the 1830s. He made the survey of the area and drew up the town plan for the city of St. Joseph.

Before the Civil War, St. Joseph was the most important city on the upper Missouri. In 1859 Friedrich Muench described a growing city with good streets and gas lighting. It had about

Musical groups like the Florence Cornet Band, Morgan County, c. 1909, were common in settlements with substantial German populations. They allowed people with similar interests to get together and provide entertainment for the entire community. A German proverb says, "Music washes the soul of care." (A. E. Schroeder Collection, courtesy of Ralph O. Lewis)

seven thousand inhabitants, including nearly two thousand Germans. One of its five newspapers was published in German. For their entertainment, the Germans in St. Joseph had organized three music societies. Muench reported that they were generally well off and got along well with their American neighbors.

Towns in the Kansas City area, including Independence, Westport, Weston, and Kansas City, were important outfitting centers in the 1850s for wagon trains heading west for California, Oregon, and New Mexico. About two thousand of the area's ten thousand inhabitants were German. Kansas City had both a German newspaper and a German-English school before the end of the 1850s. Weston had a large distillery, several wagon factories, two breweries, and five churches, two of which were German. Germans there owned some of the most important businesses, and they organized a music club and other social groups.

A delivery truck and driver of the William Volker Company. Many German immigrants were employed by Volker, who was born in Germany in 1859 and established a successful business in Kansas City. For many years Volker supported the needy, education, the arts, health sciences, and many public projects in Kansas City. All this was done so quietly that he was called "Mr. Anonymous." (Courtesy of the Western Historical Manuscript Collection–Kansas City, William Volker Company Records, KC059/N1)

By the beginning of the Civil War, the German influence throughout the state had changed the state's political and cultural life. Their love of music and gardens, their regard for education and newspapers, and many of their Christmas customs had spread to their non-German neighbors. The opposition of German immigrants to slavery helped shift the balance of political power in the state. Whether they settled in German communities or primarily English-speaking areas, the German immigrants made many contributions to frontier Missouri.

16

Know-Nothings and Forty-Eighters

Down with crowns and thrones.
—Slogan of some Forty-Eighters

The growing numbers of new immigrants began to alarm some Americans whose ancestors had arrived earlier. New arrivals began to outnumber native-born Americans in some cities. Many people became hostile toward immigrants because they saw them as a threat to American values. These conditions helped produce an antiforeign movement called "nativism." Because members of nativist groups were sworn to secrecy and refused to answer questions about their activities, they were often called "Know-Nothings."

At the national level, Know-Nothings tried to put severe limitations on immigrants. "Only Americans shall rule Americans," was their slogan. They tried to lengthen the time required for citizenship from five years to twenty-one years and to prevent immigrants from ever holding elected office. They tried to keep the poor and Catholics out of the country entirely.

Although events in Missouri were mild compared to what happened in some other states, Germans in St. Louis and other towns were persecuted by members of the nativist movement. Friedrich Muench ranked nativism as second only to slavery as a "damnable abuse of social life."

The tension in Missouri sometimes turned violent. In 1836 a mob threatened the officers of the first German-language newspaper in St. Louis, the *Anzeiger des Westens*. The mob was angry because the paper's editor, Wilhelm Weber, had strongly protested the murder of a black man named Francis McIntosh.

The Germans escaped harm from this mob, but they were not always so fortunate.

In 1852 violence broke out in St. Louis between the Know-Nothings and the German-Americans in a controversy over the election for mayor. Germans seized control of a polling place to prevent their opponents from voting. A crowd of some five thousand people marched from the center of the city to recapture it. A riot followed. One person was killed, and a German tavern was burned down in the uproar.

Nativists also sought power in government. In the mid-1840s the nativists won control of city government in St. Louis and banned public transportation after 2 P.M. on Sunday. This was aimed at immigrants who used Sunday as a day of recreation. Without public transportation, many of the Germans were unable to go to parks or beer gardens to enjoy their one day off work.

In 1855 Washington King, a Know-Nothing, was elected mayor of St. Louis. His administration adopted Sunday closing laws and enforced them in Irish pubs and German beer gardens. This was even more effective in limiting the Germans' social activities on Sunday afternoons than the ban on public transportation.

In 1861 newly elected police commissioners attempted to prohibit theater performances on Sunday, the day German theater attracted its largest crowds. The commissioners had advised Heinrich Boernstein not to open his theater on Sunday, April 14; he opened it anyway. Just before the production was to begin, the police chief and forty policemen arrived to close the theater. There was almost a riot, but Boernstein canceled the show and urged the crowd to leave quietly.

Boernstein was called a "Forty-Eighter" because he came to America after the 1848 revolution in Germany. In 1848, revolutions swept through nearly every country in Europe. When the attempt to unite Germany into a more democratic society failed, many of these revolutionaries fled for their lives. Several settled in St. Louis.

These political refugees brought with them strongly held democratic ideals that they had developed in their struggles against the aristocracies of Europe. The Forty-Eighters were generally better educated, more liberal, and more politically active

Carl Schurz, one of the refugees from the Revolution of 1848, is shown here during his student days in Germany. He became an important journalist and political figure in Missouri and nationally, and was one of the most famous of all the German immigrants. (A. E. Schroeder Collection, Western Historical Manuscript Collection–Columbia)

than most of the earlier immigrants. They were important to the development of German cultural and educational institutions, and they made a significant impact on the larger American culture as well.

One of the most notable of the Forty-Eighters to come to St. Louis was Carl Schurz, who had a distinguished career as a politician and journalist. Schurz helped elect Abraham Lincoln to the presidency by persuading hundreds of thousands of German-Americans to vote for the Republican Party in 1860. He opposed slavery and fought in the Union army, where he won the rank of major general. From 1865 to 1868 he worked as a journalist, and for a time he published the *St. Louis Westliche Post*. In 1869 he was elected to represent Missouri in the United States Senate, where he began to work against corruption in government. In 1877 Schurz was appointed to serve as secretary of the interior for President Rutherford B. Hayes and began the development of the national park system. While secretary of the interior he also introduced the idea of a merit system for public employees. Throughout his career Schurz defended newly arrived immigrants in his writing and speeches.

In spite of some serious obstacles, German immigrants who came to Missouri in the mid-1800s made important contributions to American society.

17

Germans Fight in the Civil War

Ven I comes from der Deutsche Countree, I vorks
somedimes at baking,
Und den I runs a beer-saloon, und den I tries shoe-
making.
But now I march mit musket out to safe dot Yankee
Eagle.
Dey dress me up in soldier's clothes to go and fight
mit Sigel.
—John F. Poole,
"I Goes to Fight mit Sigel"

The Germans in Missouri played a vital role in the early days
of the Civil War. Because of their strong support of the Union and
their opposition to slavery, they were quick to respond when
Missouri's Southern sympathizers attempted to take the state
into the Confederacy.

One of the most important events of the Civil War in Missouri took place in St. Louis on May 10, 1861. The Missouri State
Guard had set up a camp, which they named Camp Jackson
in honor of Missouri's governor, Claiborne Fox Jackson. Union
supporters feared that the troops at Camp Jackson would capture
the weapons in the U.S. arsenal in the city, because it did not have
an adequate defense. U.S. military leaders supplied weapons to
groups of Germans who were loyal to the Union and allowed
them to move into the arsenal.

On the morning of May 10 the Union commander, Captain
Nathaniel Lyon, gave the order for the German Home Guard
forces to march on Camp Jackson. They marched by several
routes and completely surrounded the camp. The State Guard

commander, General Daniel Frost, recognized the impossible situation his troops were in and surrendered.

The militia were marched out as prisoners to be taken to the arsenal. However, Captain Lyon was kicked by a horse shortly after the surrender, and no one seemed to be in charge. As a result, the German soldiers were forced to stand with their prisoners for several hours while a crowd gathered, much of it hostile to the Germans. There were shouts of "Hurrah for Jeff Davis," and "Damn the Dutch." Rocks and other objects were thrown at the troops.

Eyewitness accounts of what happened next differ. It seems that someone in the crowd fired several shots, wounding one of the German officers. As the Union troops began their march back to the arsenal, incidents occurred at several points. At one location, people in the crowd threw stones at the soldiers. Someone fired a pistol, killing one man and wounding Captain Constantin Blandowski in the knee. He died from the wound the next day.

Before Blandowski was wounded, the German troops apparently fired several shots over the crowd. When the captain was hit, however, some fired into the crowd. A number of people, perhaps as many as twenty-eight, were killed. Some of those killed were simply bystanders, watching the events out of curiosity.

One man who was barely missed by bullets fired over the crowd was William Tecumseh Sherman. He was there watching the scene with his young son. General Sherman later led some of the St. Louis German troops in his march through Georgia.

The capture of Camp Jackson was an extremely important event in the attempt to keep Missouri in the Union. The loyalty of Missouri officials to the Union had been in doubt after the election of President Abraham Lincoln in 1860. It was a state with a history of strong Southern, pro-slavery sympathies.

Missouri had entered the Union in 1821 as a slave state. However, even on the eve of the Civil War in 1860, it did not have a large number of slave owners. Slaves were concentrated in two main areas: in the counties along the Mississippi north of St. Louis, and those north of the Missouri from Callaway County to the Kansas border. The slaveholding area in central Missouri is still known as "Little Dixie."

Louis Benecke emigrated from Stiege in the Harz Mountains to Missouri in 1856. He is shown here in 1862 as a sergeant in the Union army. He founded the first public school in Brunswick, Missouri, a thriving nineteenth-century river port with a lively social and cultural life. Benecke practiced law in Brunswick, became active in local and state politics, and wrote several handbooks promoting immigration to Chariton County. (Benecke Family Collection, Western Historical Manuscript Collection–Columbia)

Some Missourians with Southern sympathies didn't like the Germans. These negative feelings were increased by the events surrounding the capture of Camp Jackson in St. Louis. (State Historical Society of Missouri, Columbia)

Governor Jackson and most members of the state legislature elected in 1860 supported the rights of slaveholders. They wanted Missouri to join the Southern states leaving the Union. But the majority of Missourians did not want to join the South. When Jackson called for a state convention to decide the issue of Missouri's secession from the Union, the popular vote was heavily in favor of staying with the Union. Even though the people's will to remain in the Union was clear, it took military action to enforce that will. Missouri's Germans played a vital role in that effort.

Most German immigrants believed strongly in the ideals of individual liberty. They opposed slavery and had no sympathy for the Southern cause. Nine of the ten regiments of volunteers raised in St. Louis were primarily German. Germans from Missouri, including Peter J. Osterhaus and Franz Sigel, were prominent military leaders during the Civil War.

General Franz Sigel. A Civil War broadside celebrated his fame, but mis-spelled his name. "There is a General in the West whose deeds have come to fame / He is a gallant soldier, and in movements he is game; / Then let us raise our voices high and give three hearty cheers / For Siegel, hero of the West, and his German volunteers."—Stanza from "Our German Volunteers." (State Historical Society of Missouri, Columbia)

While many of the German volunteers had noble motives, others did not. Some believed that the war provided an opportunity to prove the Germans' worth. They could demonstrate their loyalty to their new country to everyone. They wanted to counteract the slurs against "the Dutch," as they were called. As one recruit explained, "The main thing . . . was that each one was eager to teach the German-haters a never-to-be-forgotten lesson."

In fact, not all Missouri Germans were antislavery. Some even owned slaves. John Buegel of St. Louis reported his surprise on his return to the city after several months of service in the Union army to learn how strong Southern sympathies were among the Saxon Lutherans there. In general, however, Germans both opposed slavery and supported the Union.

Although other Missourians made fun of the German soldiers because of their broken English and their reputation for drinking beer, the Missouri Germans were proud of their role in helping keep Missouri with the Union.

18

A German Soldier's Story

All who valued their lives sought shelter as quickly
as possible.
    —John Buegel,
    Diary

War often brings bonds of friendship among the troops who
suffer through its hardships together. A young German soldier
from St. Louis named John Buegel kept a diary throughout the
Civil War years. He recorded the war through the eyes of an
ordinary soldier.

Buegel remembered his first Christmas in the army, spent
at Rolla in 1861. When the weather turned cold two weeks before Christmas, he and his three tent mates decided to build a
log house so they would have better shelter. He quarried stone
for a fireplace while they cut and trimmed logs. They built a
small cabin and moved in before Christmas. They celebrated
the holiday with a shipment of provisions sent by the family
of one: "a few flasks of wine, a small keg of the best beer, fifty
cigars, a few packages of tobacco, sausages, ham, cheese and
other delicacies." They were ordered to move to another location
on the first day of February, so they were not able to enjoy their
cabin for long.

Sometimes it seemed they were ordered to march for no
reason at all. One day in December four companies of men with
two cannons were ordered to march from Rolla to the Gasconade
River, a distance of about twelve miles. After they had seen
the river and eaten some of the hard bread they carried with
them, they were ordered to return to their camp at Rolla. Buegel
commented in his diary that perhaps they were meant to learn
to swim, but the water was too cold and wet. "So we had just
learned to walk," he said.

John Buegel's Civil War diary begins with a drawing that shows the patriotism he felt. In spite of his noble intentions, he was sometimes very critical of the behavior of his officers. (Western Historical Manuscript Collection–Columbia)

In the summer of 1861, Franz Sigel, commander of the Second Brigade of the Missouri Volunteers, led his troops against a rebel force at Carthage. Sigel's much smaller brigade was not able to defeat the rebels, but he was able to slow their movement enough so that Nathaniel Lyon could bring troops to Springfield to join Sigel's men. The battle of Wilson's Creek south of Springfield was one of the bloodiest in Missouri.

Buegel, serving under Sigel's command at Wilson's Creek, recalled later that his regiment had been held for five hours without attacking the enemy. Meanwhile, the rebels were moving their guns to nearby hills. Once there, the guns opened a devastating fire. Many of the German soldiers were killed, including Friedrich Muench's son Berthold, and the rest were driven from the field.

General Sigel's actions at Carthage and Wilson's Creek were criticized in a song that remained popular in the Missouri Ozarks for more than a hundred years.

Old Sigel fought some all that day
But lost his army in the fray
And off old Sigel he did run
With two Dutch guards but ne'er a gun.

Sigel was more successful later against the Confederate forces at Pea Ridge in Arkansas.

Buegel was able to maintain his sense of patriotism throughout more than three years of service in the Union army, but he saw some events through the eyes of a cynic. After months of constant marching and fighting rebels, including the major battle at Pea Ridge, Buegel commented, "We were all so run down by hardship, that we had more rheumatism than patriotism."

During the Civil War 620,000 Union and Confederate soldiers lost their lives. They died from disease, malnutrition, exposure to extreme weather conditions, and injury. Those who survived suffered terrible hardships. The Civil War was fought mainly by volunteer soldiers on both sides who fought for freedom as they understood it.

For the soldiers who fought with the North, including many of German origin, the Union represented the ideals of liberty. The nineteenth-century immigrants to the United States had left a world ruled by emperors, kings, and princes to come to a democratic republic in the New World. These immigrants and their sons were willing to lay down their lives for the Union. One soldier from St. Charles explained that he had come to this country because he admired America's free institutions, and he did not want to let "this free republic" be broken up.

The Civil War tested the strength of the Union, but in the end the nation was preserved. John Buegel and other immigrant soldiers, with both patriotism *and* rheumatism, did their part to save the democracy they had adopted as their new home.

Both Dr. Bernhard Bruns and his son, Heinrich, supported the Union cause and died during the Civil War. Heinrich lost his life at Iuka, Mississippi, on July 7, 1863, the first soldier from Jefferson City to die in battle in the Civil War. Dr. Bruns was a major and served as a medical officer. He died of illness April 1, 1864. (Painting by Jerry Berneche)

19

Plain Living and Plain Food

Fettbrot: a piece of bread spread with lard and sprinkled with sugar, an after-school snack.

In the second half of the nineteenth century, new German immigrants continued to be drawn to cities and towns in Missouri where their countrymen had settled earlier. New German settlements continued to be formed, too.

Not long after the Civil War, a group of German Baptists moved from Rockingham County, Virginia, to Ray County, Missouri. They founded a new town, which they called Rockingham, and established the Church of the Brethren there. In the 1870s, Lowry City in St. Clair County, Freistatt in Lawrence County, White Church in Howell County, and a German community near Martinsburg in Montgomery County were settled. White Church and Martinsburg drew many settlers from Westphalia in Osage County.

One of the early preachers in Rockingham was Samuel Bowman Shirky. He was born in 1840 and grew up on a Virginia farm. The Shirky family belonged to a religious group that is sometimes called Dunkards, because they practice baptism by immersing, or dipping, adults three times. They believed in "plain living, plain dress, plain food and temperance."

In 1865 Samuel Shirky married Catharine Zigler, a neighbor from Rockingham County, Virginia. They moved to Missouri in the spring of 1869 and settled in Ray County, where they had eight children and built a large and prosperous farm. By the early 1870s the settlement of Dunkards in Ray County measured about ten miles by ten miles. Converts were made from a number of English-speaking families, but the German influence remained strong.

Not all Germans were Unionists. Many old immigrants in the southeastern and southern states supported the Confederacy when their states seceded from the Union. Samuel Shirky, one of the founders of Rockingham, Missouri, served in the Confederate army during the Civil War. (Courtesy of James Shirky)

Much of the work on the farms in the community was shared. The men worked together in harvesting, butchering, and building. The women shared the work of quilting, canning, and cooking. In 1908 the church allowed its members to wear modern clothes, as long as they were modest and without decoration. Many of the older people continued to wear traditional black or brown clothing into the 1940s.

James M. Shirky, great-grandson of Samuel and Catharine Shirky, remembered that a typical Dunkard meal required a great amount of work "by way of the garden, the berry patch, the smokehouse, the milkhouse, the cellar, the chicken house, the barn and the pantry."

James Shirky's grandmother used one thousand pounds of flour a year to bake all the foods required for proper Dunkard meals. This is a typical meal his grandmother would fix:

1. chicken noodle soup
2. ham and apple dumplings
3. potatoes
4. candied sweet potatoes
5. steamed cabbage
6. lima beans
7. peas
8. squash
9. corn fritters
10. cherries
11. sliced tomatoes
12. peaches
13. sweet rolls
14. molasses crumb pie
15. angel cake
16. cinnamon buns with coffee and tea.

Shirky remembers his childhood being old-fashioned, but filled with great happiness. Unfortunately, during the years when he was growing up on the farm, the Dunkard community was being devastated by the Great Depression. Many families lost their farms during the Depression years, and some were forced into the world outside the community to work. The community never fully recovered from these difficult years.

Freistatt is another good example of a later German settlement in Missouri. In the early 1870s, several families from Minnesota, Wisconsin, and Illinois built a new town on the southern edge of Lawrence County. They selected this site because the Frisco Railroad was selling the land to homesteaders for six dollars an acre.

Some of these settlers were immigrants, while others were second- or third-generation Americans. They had come from different regions in Germany, but they were all Lutheran. Because there were no Lutheran churches in the area where they were planning to settle, some of the men stopped in St. Louis and asked officials of the Lutheran Church if they could send a pastor to visit them from time to time.

The early worship services were held in the homes of the settlers. When a pastor was not there, one of the men read from a book of sermons. The service also included singing and discussing a lesson.

By 1878 there were twenty-four students in the Freistatt school, which was held in the church building. The first full-time teacher, Mr. Nehrling, was paid three hundred dollars a year and given a free home and a supply of firewood.

Herman Biermann was Freistatt's first postmaster and the owner of the Biermann General Merchandise Store. The store served as a meeting place for the people in the town. At the store they could pick up their mail; buy groceries, beer, clothing and other items; and sell rabbits that were shipped to Chicago. Herman Biermann's son, A. H. Biermann, served as postmaster until he retired in 1967.

Weddings in Freistatt were major community events. They usually took place in the church on Sunday afternoon. The reception was held at the home of the bride's parents, and included cookies, soda, and beer in the afternoon followed by an evening meal. The meal took place early so that the dairy farmers, sometimes including the bridegroom, could go home and milk the

German traditions continued for many decades in some areas. This November 8, 1936, Freistatt wedding party of Bertha and Oscar Voskamp shows the custom of "wedding inviters," young men who personally invited guests to the wedding. The *Gastbitter* recited a poem in German and those who accepted the invitation fastened a ribbon, kept in the house for that purpose, to his hat or coat. (A. E. Schroeder Collection, Western Historical Manuscript Collection–Columbia, courtesy of Bertha and Oscar Voskamp)

cows. After the chores were finished, the guests returned to the reception.

Each table at the meal would be set with eight plates of beef, potatoes, pork and beans, fruit, pickles, bread, cheese, and sausage. Here is a "wedding reception recipe" for a 1930 wedding that took place at Trinity Lutheran Church in Freistatt:

1. 200 pounds of beef
2. 7 three-gallon buckets of peeled potatoes
3. 100 loaves of white bread
4. 60 loaves of rye bread
5. 1 gallon vinegar

Freistatt weddings, like German weddings everywhere, celebrated the occasion with music, food, and drink. For this 1905 wedding, the bride wore a black dress, a custom that was followed in Perry County and other areas settled by Europeans. (A. E. Schroeder Collection, Western Historical Manuscript Collection–Columbia, courtesy of Orville Osterloh)

6. 39 cans of pork and beans
7. 25 pounds of prunes
8. 15 pounds of apricots
9. 20 pounds of butter
10. 10 pounds of coffee
11. 100 cakes; 10 each of the following: angel food, sunshine, spice, applesauce, walnut, coconut, checkerboard, devil's food, chocolate marble, and banana
12. 4 gallons of pickles.

For many years, the people of Freistatt had little contact with people in other communities. In general, the men went into the town of Monett only to buy building supplies and machinery. Because of their isolation, their German heritage remained very strong. Today the residents of Freistatt still celebrate their heritage with an August Festival that draws visitors from throughout the Midwest.

German culture flourished throughout Missouri after the Civil War, not just in isolated small towns. Many German men became influential in state and local politics. German businesses prospered, helping build the state's industrial economy. Some historians call the period from after the Civil War until the beginning of World War I the Golden Age of German Culture in Missouri.

20

German Life in St. Louis

Where there is singing
there you can rest.
Bad men have no songs.
  —Motto of many singing societies,
  attributed to Martin Luther

A century ago some neighborhoods in St. Louis looked like sections of cities in Germany. The streets were lined with two-story brick houses with green shutters on the windows and roofs with decorative triangular gables. On Saturday mornings German housewives could be seen scrubbing the stone steps and sometimes even the sidewalk in front of the houses.

The Germans brought their ideas of entertainment to St. Louis. The city had many public parks and gardens, supported chiefly by the Germans. Statues of German writers and statesmen were put in the parks. The gardens had trees and beautiful flowers, but they were also important for social events. Orchestras, bands, and singing societies gave concerts, and plays were held in the gardens. The owners of private parks often served beer, wine, and sausages.

On Sundays the gardens teemed with people. The Germans wanted to celebrate their one day off work in public gatherings. Sunday afternoon was a time for plays, music, and sharing food and drink. These Sunday activities brought the Germans into bitter disputes with some of the other residents of the city who did not approve of beer-drinking and the German style of relaxing. Many Americans believed that Sunday should be a quiet day spent in worship and reflection.

Music was important to the Germans who settled in St. Louis. Many of the German immigrants brought a piano or another musical instrument to their new country. They introduced the idea of playing the piano in the home to their American neighbors.

The first choral group in St. Louis was formed by a group of men from a brewery. Later, the German American community supported the establishment of the St. Louis Symphony Orchestra. Most of the first musicians in the orchestra were German.

The first German theater performance in St. Louis was a production of *The Robbers,* by the German playwright, poet, and historian Friedrich Schiller. Schiller often wrote about human dignity and spiritual freedom, and he was greatly admired by many German Americans. The play was performed in 1842 in a hotel dining room and was received enthusiastically by the audience. The money raised from the production provided aid to a German actor who had arrived in the city without any money.

The actor, named Riese, played the main character in the play. The other roles were played by amateurs, but unfortunately no woman could be found to play the role of the heroine, Amalie. This character is essential to the play's final scene, where Amalie is stabbed to death. Just before the last act, Riese positively refused to continue without an Amalie, so the hotel's cook was hastily dressed in a white gown and pushed on stage. When she did not fall to the floor at the right time, witnesses report that Riese gave the poor woman "a mighty blow" that knocked her to the floor.

One way German Americans maintained their German culture was through social organizations. There were more than three hundred German societies of one kind or another in St. Louis in the years before World War I, not including church-related groups. More than twenty still remain active.

The Germans formed societies to appeal to every social and economic class. The Liederkranz Club was only open to the social elite. In 1907, the club had eight hundred members and built a black marble and brick building with a banquet hall, a concert hall, a ballroom, a bowling room, card and billiard rooms, a reading room, a café, and a garden.

Clubs that were open to more people were more common. There were singing societies, groups that provided aid to the needy, shooting societies, clubs for immigrants from the same

Caroline Langhauser is shown sweeping the outside steps of her home in St. Louis. This practice contributed to the Germans' reputation for cleanliness. (A. E. Schroeder Collection, Western Historical Manuscript Collection–Columbia, courtesy of Elenore Schewe)

Beer gardens like this one in St. Louis featured entertainment for the whole family and attracted large crowds. (State Historical Society of Missouri, Columbia)

region in the German states, entertainment clubs, labor unions, political groups, and Turner Societies.

Unlike the Liederkranz Club, the Turners were a cross section of the entire German community, including men and women, rich and poor, young and old. The Turners were organized in Germany in 1811 to promote physical education and intellectual pursuits. Several Turner Societies were formed in the St. Louis area. Often they had buildings with gyms, libraries, and rooms for classes or lectures. The Turners introduced the idea of teaching physical education in schools and later began the movement to create public playgrounds.

Festival days helped maintain and celebrate the city's German heritage. A ten-day festival, commemorating Schiller's life, held in May 1905 included a parade in which eight thousand people marched through streets decorated with American and German flags and pictures of Schiller. After the parade, thirty thousand people gathered in a park to listen to music, singing, poems, and speeches in German and English.

The St. Louis Music Hall was the site of many concerts. The German community supported music and theater in St. Louis. (A. E. Schroeder Collection, Western Historical Manuscript Collection–Columbia)

At the turn of the century, St. Louis was one of the leading cultural and educational cities in the nation, with its fine symphony orchestra, two major universities, one of the most important botanical gardens in the nation, and six daily newspapers. Two of these were German-language papers with national influence. Many people saw St. Louis as a kind of German city in the middle of America.

21

Village Society

It seemed that any where there were at least three
Germans they formed a society.
—Audrey L. Olson,
"The Nature of an Immigrant
Community"

Whether they settled in St. Louis or in villages, the Germans believed that life should be enjoyed. Even in small towns, they formed many kinds of social organizations. Some provided a variety of activities; others focused on specific interests like music. In Hermann there were two shooting clubs established in the first year of the town's existence. Such local clubs sponsored many events for members and their families.

A chapter of the Turners was organized in Washington in 1859 and reorganized when many of its members returned from the Civil War. The Washington Turners began a singing society in 1865 and a drama society three years later. The drama group presented about two plays each month for the community's entertainment. The Turners sponsored regular Sunday evening family gatherings, and special events such as a *Kinderball* (a dance for children) in December and a New Year's Eve celebration that included a play, music, and dancing until dawn.

Because of their love of music, many early German settlers brought musical instruments to Missouri villages. The Latin farmers who settled around Dutzow regularly gathered in Wilhelm Bock's home for an afternoon of music and singing. Dr. Bruns bought a piano for Jette in 1837 from the Hesse family when they decided to return to Germany.

Musical organizations were formed in villages, too. In their first year in Hermann the settlers formed a brass band. In the 1840s they formed singing societies. In Augusta a singing society

Smaller towns did not always have the ability to have large orchestras, but music was kept alive by small groups such as the Schwaller Band in Westphalia. (A. E. Schroeder Collection, Western Historical Manuscript Collection–Columbia, courtesy of Ed Bode)

was formed in 1856. The group held its first *Maifest,* or May festival, that year. John Fuhr, a shoemaker in the town, had been trained in music, and he became the first president of the organization.

Fuhr taught vocal and instrumental music to both adults and children. He was born in Darmstadt in the German province of Hesse in 1820. He had come to Missouri in 1837, moving to Augusta in 1848. In addition to his musical talents, he was a farmer for a short time before opening a shoemaking shop. His business expanded to include wine making; he produced about twenty-eight hundred barrels of wine a year. Eventually he employed about a dozen workers.

The kind of music the Germans liked was different from that of their American neighbors. At dances in Washington in the 1830s before many Germans had arrived, the music was usually provided by a single fiddler. Gert Goebel, one of the first Germans to settle in the town, described a dance where two fiddlers

The Turner Societies included members from all parts of the community. The very active Turners in Washington, Missouri, included this group of women and their teachers in 1897. (State Historical Society of Missouri, Columbia)

played. The two tried to play the same tune, but one played more slowly than the other. The American crowd was not bothered by the problem, but actually enjoyed the attempt of the faster fiddler to get further and further ahead of his partner. The crowd applauded him when he finished the tune well ahead of the other.

Goebel also told of a Virginia doctor visiting Washington in the 1850s when the town was almost entirely German. By then the immigrants had formed a small classical music orchestra. When the doctor heard the orchestra play, he was amazed that the musicians played different parts, with a violin taking the melody, for example, while other instruments played various harmonies.

The Germans also valued beautiful things for their homes. The furniture in the German farmhouses was often highly decorated, painted with bright colors. Even gardens could become works of art. Once families were settled, the garden with its beautiful flowers planted among the cabbages and salad greens became the pride of many of the German women.

The Germans' social nature embraced American activities, including baseball. Many small towns such as Concordia supported teams. Concordia was founded after Heinrich Dierking settled near there in the 1830s and wrote his friends in Hanover that there was good land available in the area. The town grew, and in 1884 St. Paul's Lutheran College offered its first classes there. (Lloyd and Nyla Shepard)

The towns they built came to resemble what they had left behind. Friedrich Muench noted that German settlements in Missouri looked like German villages, with vegetable gardens behind many houses. One town was described by a visitor as a community "of white homes with peony, rose and dahlia gardens in front, and neat orchards and vegetable plots in the rear."

The Germans of these small Missouri towns preserved much of what was best of their traditions and culture, while embracing the political freedoms offered by their new homeland. They were in the process of becoming Americans. At the same time they were changing America with their hard work and love of life, their gardens, food, beer, and wine.

22

Practical Men and Politicians

There is still a lot of trash in politics. . . . I often wonder how such important matters are treated so very simply. We miss Senator Muench. It is embarrassing that St. Charles County voted him out.
—Jette Geisberg Bruns,
Letter, 1867

In addition to the vital role Germans played in keeping Missouri in the Union, they and their descendants made significant contributions in Missouri politics in other ways, serving as local officials, state and federal lawmakers, and judges. Dr. Bernhard Bruns served as mayor of Jefferson City during the Civil War. Gert Goebel, who came to Missouri at age eighteen with the Giessen Society, served in the state legislature with Friedrich Muench and other Germans. Carl Schurz was elected to represent Missouri in the U.S. Senate only two years after he came to the state. Hugo Muench, youngest son of Friedrich, had a distinguished career as a judge of the Circuit Court of St. Louis. He was also a member of the St. Louis school board.

Arnold Krekel was another German immigrant who became a successful judge. He arrived in St. Charles County with his father when he was about sixteen. His mother had died of cholera during their journey. Krekel could not speak a word of English, but he began to study it at once. He worked as a farmhand, earning twenty-five cents for every one hundred fence rails he made. When he had saved enough money to pay his expenses at school, he attended St. Charles College. After he graduated, he studied law, and then began to practice law in St. Charles. Later he became a judge on the U.S. Western District Court in Kansas City and gained a national reputation for his decisions.

Friedrich Muench was educated in Germany to be a minister, and he was very active in public life in Missouri. His farm not only provided food and income for his family but also was a place that gave him great pleasure. (Ed Italo photograph of a painting by Theodor Bruere, c. 1850, courtesy of Elsa Muench Hunstein)

One of the most notable successes was Friedrich Muench, who became a successful farmer, teacher, political leader, and writer. His book, *The State of Missouri, An Account with Special Reference to German Immigration*, was published in Germany in 1859 to assist his countrymen who were thinking of emigrating. Unlike Duden's earlier book, it was based on twenty-four years of experience in Missouri and was filled with practical information about farming, climate, health conditions, population of the state, and much more.

Muench gave Duden much of the credit for bringing large numbers of Germans to Missouri, but others credit Muench himself with having a significant influence on potential German emigrants. Muench's writings were well known all over Germany, and he clearly wanted a large number of German immigrants to settle in Missouri, partly in the hope of changing it from a slaveholding state sympathetic to Southern political goals into a free state. Muench's goal was accomplished, but only just in time to save Missouri for the Union when the Civil War broke out.

In addition to his influence on immigration, he was an important figure in state politics, serving as a state senator from 1862 to 1865. He was also widely recognized as a leading German intellectual in America. His religious and philosophical writings were well known both here and in Germany.

Although he had grown up to a life of ideas rather than physical labor, he took great pride in his farm with its large orchards and vineyards, and became an authority on grape culture. He gave newcomers advice on farming practices and other skills needed to survive on the frontier. He died in his vineyard with his pruning hook in his hands on a sunny autumn morning in 1881, apparently a contented old man.

23

Brewing and Wine Making

> Persons who reside here [shall] be allowed to take
> up vacant lots belonging to the town . . . upon the
> following conditions . . . that each person pledge
> himself within two years to plant two-fifths of the
> lots with vines, so that in five years all the lots will
> be planted.
> —Trustees of Hermann,
> Resolution, 1844

One of the economic success stories of the Missouri Germans is due in large part to Friedrich Muench, his brother Georg, and other Latin Farmers who began the state's wine industry. Dutzow was one of the first towns to have a winery, with Augusta and Hermann close behind. In 1848, only ten years after the founding of Hermann, the town's wineries were producing ten thousand gallons of wine annually, and the town held its first *Weinfest* (wine festival) that year.

Wine production slowed down during the Civil War, but the business boomed in the 1870s and 1880s. By the early years of the twentieth century, the area around Augusta had eleven wineries. Stone Hill Winery in Hermann was the second largest winery in America and third largest in the world. Wines from Stone Hill won many international awards. Other German towns in Missouri that had wineries included Altenburg, Boonville, Freeburg, Westphalia, and Wittenberg. Missouri became the second-largest wine-producing state in the nation.

One of the first people to grow grapes at Hermann was Martin Husmann, a schoolteacher who was drawn to Missouri by the work of Gottfried Duden. His son, George Husmann, was influential in the development of the wine industry in Missouri and beyond. He and his partner, Charles Manwaring, built up one of the largest mail-order nurseries in the United States and the most profitable business in Gasconade County. In 1866 Husmann published a book on raising grapes and making wine, and a few years later he founded *The Grape Culturist,* the only journal on grape growing and wine making in the country at that time. Husmann ended his career in the state of California, where he managed a vineyard, made prize-winning wines, and continued his research and writing.

The Missouri wine industry has been important for more than its production of wines. In the 1870s when the vineyards in France were threatened by a pest that destroyed the roots of the French grapes, Missouri came to the aid of the French wine makers. The state already had more land planted in vineyards than the entire country of France. Railroad cars filled with healthy grape cuttings were shipped to France to replace those that had been destroyed. Without that help, French vineyards and wineries would have been devastated. To show its appreciation, France awarded the Cross of the French Legion of Honor to Hermann Jaeger, the man who organized the shipment. Jaeger was a Swiss-German who lived in Newton County. Grape growers from Hermann were among those who sent healthy grape roots to France.

German immigrants also made brewing beer one of Missouri's largest industries. Jacques St. Vrain opened the first brewery in St. Louis in 1810. He hired a German brewer, Victor Habb, to make "strong beer" and "table beer."

A German immigrant named Adam Lemp opened a brewery in St. Louis in 1840. He made lager beer, which became so popular that it eventually became the standard American beer. By 1860 St. Louis had forty breweries, with hundreds of employees. Many small towns had their own breweries. There were many beer gardens in St. Louis and in German towns throughout the state.

Two well-known German businessmen in St. Louis, whose names are known all over the world today, were Eberhard Anheuser and his son-in-law Adolphus Busch. Anheuser was the owner of a brewery in Bavaria. Busch grew up in a wine merchant's family in Mainz. Anheuser was a soap manufacturer in St. Louis when he took possession of a small, bankrupt brewery in 1860. Together he and Busch produced Budweiser beer by the

Edward J. Kemper was the son of one of George Husmann's friends, Christopher Kemper. Husmann took an interest in the young Kemper and encouraged him to attend the University of Missouri to study plant propagation. In 1897 Edward took over his father's business and established Hermann Grape Nurseries, which shipped healthy grapestock to growers in France and throughout the United States. As this self-portrait shows, Kemper was a serious and gifted photographer, who left a record of daily life and work in the Hermann area. (Kemper Collection, courtesy of Anna Kemper Hesse)

hundreds of thousands of barrels in the 1870s. The brewery was the first in the nation to bottle beer extensively for sale outside its local market. By the time a new brewhouse was finished in 1893, Anheuser-Busch was advertising itself as the largest brewery in the world.

The beer and wine industries were nearly destroyed in the 1920s when Prohibition made it illegal to make or sell alcoholic beverages. Many businesses closed and never reopened. It took

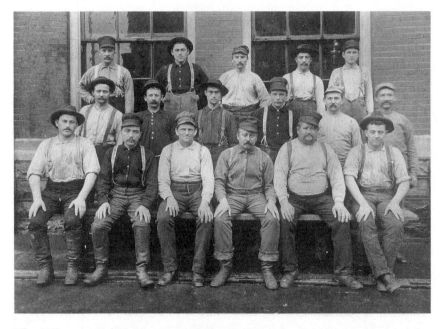

The Anheuser-Busch Brewing Association. Breweries provided many jobs, both directly and through related businesses that produced supplies such as barrels or provided services transporting and selling the beer. They supported regional agriculture through the purchase of raw materials for the brewing process. Places of work also provided the opportunity to form social organizations, such as the brewery whose workers formed the first St. Louis singing society. (Courtesy of Anheuser-Busch Corporate Archives)

many years after Prohibition ended in 1933 for the breweries and wineries to recover. Today they are again major industries for the state.

24

Millers, Merchants, and a Fine Zither Maker

> The Germans not only carry on the types of business peculiarly native to them, such as brewing, innkeeping, arts and crafts of all kinds, but also others with outstanding reliability and stability.
> —Friedrich Muench,
> *State of Missouri*

Large-scale manufacturing did not come to St. Louis until after the Civil War, but before the war there were several small German establishments with three or four employees each. A list of twenty-five early manufacturers in St. Louis shows that all were born in Germany. These early industries included lumber and flour mills; furniture, hardware, carriage and wagon making; cotton pressing and spinning; iron works; soap, chemical, and drug manufacturing; and breweries. St. Louis German immigrant Louis Epenschied supplied thousands of wagons for the Union army during the Civil War.

These early businesses grew rapidly in the economic expansion after the Civil War, and St. Louis became known as a center for flour milling, meat packing, brewing, and manufacturing furniture, hardware, chemicals, drugs, clothing, shoes, and other products. Many German immigrants were very successful financially.

Businessman Adolphus Meier is one of these success stories. Meier was born in Bremen in 1810. The son of a lawyer, he was in the shipping business as a young man. He came to St. Louis in 1837 and opened a hardware store. He exported leaf tobacco and cotton and opened the first cotton-spinning mill west of the Mississippi in 1844. Meier also owned a business that manufactured iron. By 1850 he owned one hundred thousand dollars in real estate.

There were many other German merchants in St. Louis, ranging from small shopkeepers to large-scale grain and produce commission merchants. Ernst Carl von Angelrodt ran a wholesale mercantile house and liquor business. He made a million dollars, some people said. He could be called St. Louis's first zookeeper, because he kept all kinds of American animals in his large yard, which he opened to the public on Sundays.

At the turn of the century, St. Louis was the fourth-largest city in the United States. There was still a distinct German flavor to the business community in the city at this time. The markets for St. Louis goods extended around the country. The brewing industry, dominated by Germans, was a major source of jobs and income for the city. Most of the other lines of businesses, including shipping, hardware, milling, and the manufacture of chemicals, furniture, and clothing, had at least one important German American company. In 1902 there were at least six small and medium-sized banks controlled by German Americans.

Smaller German communities also had numerous businesses. In 1888 Washington had grown to a town of about four thousand; almost all the residents were German. There were about one hundred businesses, including eleven general stores, three hardware stores, and three drug stores. Residents could add to their homemade clothes with purchases from four shoe stores and six clothing stores. They could also have clothing made by the town's two tailors and shoes by the shoemaker. In addition to these skilled craftsmen, Washington had two bakers, a butcher, a gunsmith, and three watchmakers.

Businesses in the town provided goods necessary to the area's farmers. There were two farm machinery dealers, five blacksmiths and wagon makers, four saddle and harness makers, two millers, and a grain dealer.

Travelers could find rooms at two hotels and have their meals and a drink in any of nine saloons. The photographer could take their picture while they were in town. Five doctors and two dentists took care of the medical needs of the residents. A bank and two savings associations served their financial needs.

Frederick Muehl (seated) demonstrates how the zither was played. Franz Schwarzer is at right and Mr. Schmidt holds a book. Zithers provided the music for dancing on the decks of some immigrant ships bound for America. (State Historical Society of Missouri, Columbia)

The town boasted two newspapers, one in English and one in German.

The town also had several manufacturing firms, which made cigars, brooms, horse collars, and beer. One local company, the Missouri Meerschaum Company, became famous for its corncob pipes. Franz Schwarzer's zither company was known around the world as a maker of fine musical instruments.

The zither was a very popular instrument among German people in Europe and America. Schwarzer made some of the best. At the 1873 International Exhibition in Vienna, Austria, the zither capital of the world, his zithers won the Gold Medal of Progress, the highest award given. Schwarzer zithers were sold in every major European country and in South America, as well as in the United States. When production was at its peak, the Washington

Stores like Wenger's hardware store in St. James provided necessary supplies to those living in small towns and on surrounding farms. Such stores were places where regular customers could expect to spend some time in friendly talk with shopkeepers and neighbors. (Western Historical Manuscript Collection–Columbia, courtesy of James Library)

factory employed about twenty-five workers. Before it closed it had produced more than eleven thousand instruments.

Even smaller towns had numerous businesses. New Haven, for example, had more than thirty in 1888, including various stores and skilled craftsmen. The town had three doctors. At least four of the New Haven shop owners were women.

In the last half of the 1800s, the business life of small towns was much more vital than today. The German communities in Missouri provided many services that are now available only in much larger towns.

25

World War I

The elimination of German and the universal use of English at all such gatherings [is] essential to the development of a true patriotic sentiment among all people.
—Missouri Council of Defense,
Resolution, 1918

Whether they lived in mostly German communities or in towns where they were the only German family, eventually the immigrants found it necessary to deal with the non-German society around them. Many thought they could remain German and be good Americans. Much of the time this was possible, but in times of crisis tensions often came into the open. During World War I and the Prohibition era, their loyalty was frequently tested.

World War I was a particularly troublesome period for German Americans. Before World War I Missouri had twenty-eight newspapers and twelve monthly publications printed in German. Church services were held in German throughout the state, and German schools taught the language to children and grandchildren of the German immigrants. It was common for the children of the second or third generations to speak German at home and learn English as a second language in school. Many schools conducted what is now called bilingual education, with morning classes taught in German and afternoon classes in English.

The German immigrants who came to America believed they could preserve what they valued in their own culture with the freedom allowed in the New World. They were fiercely loyal to the American ideals of freedom, democracy, and equality. However, they believed they could be good Americans and still use the German language and practice their customs in school, church, and community.

They found themselves in a difficult situation when World War I broke out in Europe in 1914. Most of the newspapers and politicians in the country were sympathetic to the British cause. Most Germans in Missouri had been either indifferent or hostile to the German government before 1914 (their loyalty had been to the culture, not the politics of Germany), but when war with England broke out their support for the fatherland was overwhelming.

Missouri Germans bought German war bonds and contributed to the German Red Cross. Richard Bartholdt, a member of Congress from Missouri, argued that Britain was trying to drive a wedge between Germany and America. While the English-language press presented the British viewpoint, the German newspapers gave the German perspective. German Americans were vitally interested in the news about the war. In Hermann people went to the train station early each morning to get the latest news from the war in the St. Louis papers.

German Americans did not believe the United States would go to war with Germany. While the nation had fought two wars against Britain, it had never fought against their homeland. However, in 1917 the unthinkable happened. After increasing tensions between the two countries, largely a result of the sinking of merchant and passenger ships by German submarines, the United States declared war on Germany.

Public support for Germany ceased immediately. While German Americans saw themselves as members of the German culture, they owed their political allegiance to the United States. The majority rallied to the American cause. They bought U.S. war bonds and their newspapers declared their political loyalty. Many young men of German descent served in the U.S. Army. General John J. Pershing, himself a Missourian of German heritage, commanded American troops in Europe. In spite of these things, sentiment against German Americans was strong during the war.

When the United States entered the war, the Missouri Council of Defense was charged with the "elimination of enemy language and influence," and the pressures against using the German language intensified. In 1918 the Council declared its opposition to the "use of the German language in schools, churches,

MISSOURI LEADS IN FOOD INCREASE

Results of 1917

MISSOURI RISES
IN RANK

1916 Value all crops. $261,269,000
1917 Value all crops 546,036,000
1916 Rank 14th
1917 Rank 5th

U. S. CROP REPORT

What for 1918

THE FARMER'S
PATRIOTISM

¶The Missouri farmers are. to be congratulated on this great achievement of 1917!

¶What for 1918?

¶The need is greater! The farmers of Missouri must rally again. More acreage and greater yields is the call of the country.

ARE WE BACK OF THE BOYS AT THE FRONT?
YES!!!

After the United States entered World War I, descendants of German immigrants joined other Missourians in the war effort. (*Final Report of the Missouri Council of Defense 1917–1918–1919*. Courtesy Donald M. Lance)

lodges, and public buildings of every character." German organizations were urged to use English as "a national duty" and as "evidence of loyalty." In Missouri and other states there were threats and incidents of violence against German Americans.

German Lutherans were hit especially hard by the hostility of the war years. German-language church services were disrupted, and pastors were threatened. This happened throughout the Midwest, partly because of the very vocal support by the Missouri Synod of the Lutheran Church for the German cause before the United States entered the war.

In some places the anti-German hostility caused absurd actions. Some advocated eliminating the Fahrenheit thermometer because of its un-American name. Sauerkraut was renamed Liberty Cabbage, and frankfurters began to be called hot dogs. The

General John J. Pershing (front row, seated), shown with his family, was commander of the American Expeditionary Force in Europe during World War I. His great-grandfather, Frederick Pershing, came to Philadelphia from Germany in 1749, working for the ship's captain to pay for his passage. Pershing's father moved to Missouri in 1858, working on flatboats on the Ohio River to earn his way. (State Historical Society of Missouri, Columbia)

Missouri Council of Defense wanted to make the use of German on telephones illegal.

In contrast to the problems caused at home, the ability of some of the soldiers to speak German served them well during the war. A story told by a soldier from central Missouri shows that sometimes it was a life-saving skill. When he was wounded on a battlefield in France, he sought shelter in a shell crater. He was cold and frightened. He knew that sometimes soldiers on both sides killed wounded enemy soldiers rather than take them prisoner. During the night he heard German soldiers moving across the battlefield, from one shell crater to another. A young German soldier appeared on the rim of the crater with a gun pointed at him, and he knew he was dead. However, when he called to the enemy soldier in German, the soldier laughed and called over his comrades. They carried the wounded Missourian back to their lines to get medical treatment.

German Americans were suspected of treason in spite of their public statements of loyalty and service in the American army. As a result, German culture was weakened. Most German American political groups had disappeared by the war's end.

English replaced German in many churches, clubs, and newspapers. During the war, for example, schools in Jefferson City and other towns stopped teaching German. In St. Louis in 1914, one-fourth of all high school students studied German. By 1922 the number had dropped to less than 1 percent. The use of German suffered in other ways. German newspapers, including the Sedalia Journal, ceased publication. In St. Louis the last German theater was closed.

The repression of German culture that took place during World War I dealt a blow to German life in Missouri from which it never recovered.

26

No Beer and No Job

[Prohibition] was the one external force that could
destroy the only type of community they had ever
known in St. Louis.
—Audrey L. Olson,
St. Louis Germans

The Prohibition movement was strengthened by the anti-German sentiment expressed during World War I. In some ways, it proved even more damaging to attempts to preserve German culture in Missouri.

Attitudes about alcohol and Sunday activities differed widely and sometimes led to serious clashes between immigrant groups and other Americans. Prohibitionists believed that alcohol was an instrument of the devil. The temperance movement was aimed at eliminating what its members saw as the evils of drink. The movement grew in strength in the last decades of the 1800s and early years of the 1900s. In 1887 the Missouri legislature passed a law allowing local governments to make it illegal to make or drink alcohol. Within two years, fifty Missouri counties had done so. Prohibitionists claimed that they were preserving the religious nature of Sunday from "foreign-born saloon keepers and brewers," a direct slap at the Germans.

The National Prohibition Act, passed after the Eighteenth Amendment to the United States Constitution was approved, went into effect in 1920. Prohibition, as the law was called, made it illegal to produce or consume alcoholic beverages in the United States. It wiped out the large grape-growing, wine-making, and brewing industries in Missouri.

In St. Louis, Prohibition threatened the jobs of some eleven thousand workers in the breweries and related industries, such as bottle makers and the coopers who made barrels for draft

Germans believed that beer was simply a part of everyday life. This ad, which proclaims that beer is "a national drink, a healthy drink, a family drink," is meant to reinforce that attitude. (A. E. Schroeder Collection, Western Historical Manuscript Collection–Columbia)

beer. Two of the city's prominent brewery owners, Otto Stifel and William Lemp Jr., took their own lives during the early years of Prohibition. Only the large breweries managed to stay in business by turning to the manufacture of other products. Anheuser-Busch made soft drinks, corn starch, syrups, and other products.

The economic disruption was severe in places like Hermann and Augusta, which relied heavily on the wineries. Vineyards were destroyed as markets for wine grapes disappeared overnight. One resident commented years later that the Great Depression, which began in 1929, had come to Hermann ten years earlier with Prohibition. The life of virtually every resident of Hermann was disrupted by the closing of the wineries.

Stone Hill Winery, the third largest in the world, converted its wine cellars to the production of mushrooms. Some breweries

This ad from a Springfield newspaper indicates the way in which the fear of Germany as the enemy in World War I was linked to the movement to prohibit the use of alcohol. It claims that "The saloon and the brewery are traitorously disloyal." (A. E. Schroeder Collection, Western Historical Manuscript Collection–Columbia)

were able to resume production when Prohibition ended in 1933. Bringing back grape and wine production was much slower, but today Missouri's wineries are again among the best in the country.

Prohibition also drastically changed German social life. The normal Sunday entertainment of families gathering in taverns, beer gardens, or wine gardens to enjoy food, drink, and music, and to talk and laugh with friends and neighbors, was impossible. Many German social organizations never recovered from the loss of attendance and revenues that they experienced during these years.

Most German Americans saw Prohibition as an example of government interference with their private lives. Something that had been a central part of everyday life for thousands was now illegal. Families could no longer send the children to the local brewery or tavern to bring home the beer for supper. Grocery stores in St. Louis had sold beer by the pail, and corner saloons were common. As historian Sister Audrey Olson puts it, these taverns were so respectable "that a father could send his daughters to buy a pail of beer, while the girls happily anticipated receiving a free German pretzel or two from the saloon keeper or his wife."

The German Americans' sense of cultural identity that had been severely damaged by the anti-German sentiments during World War I was further threatened by Prohibition. For many, their German cultural identity seemed lost forever. For some Missourians of German descent, however, the American Bicentennial in 1976 brought revived interest in their heritage.

27

Missouri's German Heritage

Was it not, in great measure, for the sake of my
children that I attempted the great undertaking?
—Friedrich Steines,
Letter, 1834

It is hard to imagine what life in Missouri today would be like
if German immigrants had never come to America and settled in
Missouri in such large numbers. Their influence continues to be
felt in all our lives today. They brought Old World customs with
them to the Missouri frontier. Many were adopted by the larger
culture and are now practiced widely throughout the state.

The Turner societies are gone, but community theater and
musical organizations continue. In many small Missouri towns,
the traditions of shooting matches and Sunday afternoon baseball
evolved from the German *Schuetzenfest* and Sunday afternoon
recreation.

Many common foods in Missouri came from the Germans.
German immigrants gave us some of our most delicious sweets
and breads, including the jelly doughnut, apple strudel, kaiser
rolls, pretzels, rye bread, and many kinds of cookies. These immigrants also brought their skills for making many different
sausages to America. Germans make more kinds of sausages than
any other nationality. Other German foods that are common in
Missouri today include apple butter, potato salad, hamburgers,
and sauerkraut.

Because Missouri's German immigrants came from many
regions of Germany, some of their Christmas traditions differed
from one community to another. However, some of the customs
they had in common, such as the Christmas tree, have been

ESTABLISHED 1852

ALCOHOL 10.5% BY VOL.

Settler's Pride

A SWEET WHITE WINE

MADE & BOTTLED BY HERMANNHOF WINERY, BW 106
330 E. FIRST ST., HERMANN, MO 65041. FOR INFORMATION ABOUT
INGREDIENTS IN THIS PRODUCT, WRITE HERMANNHOF WINERY.

This wine label recognizes the debt that wineries owe to the Germans who planted the first vineyards and began making wine more than 150 years ago. The name of the wine also shows how pride in their heritage has been passed on to the descendants of the immigrants. (A. E. Schroeder Collection, Western Historical Manuscript Collection–Columbia)

widely adopted beyond their communities. Holiday customs from Germany changed the American celebration of Christmas.

The German immigrants brought us the concept of Christmas as a family holiday. In addition to the idea of decorating an evergreen tree, they brought the traditions of giving Christmas presents and enjoying sweets as part of holiday meals. One of the most popular Christmas carols in the United States, "Silent Night," came from Austria, a German-speaking country. The custom of children hanging Christmas stockings is adapted from the celebration of St. Nicholas' Day. St. Nicholas' Day has been celebrated in Germany and other northern European countries for hundreds of years. On December 5, the evening before the festival day, children left their shoes near their beds or on a

The Christmas tree is just one of the German customs that have become a part of life in America. This tree in the Benecke home in Brunswick has decorations on and under it in typical Missouri German fashion. (Benecke Family Collection, Western Historical Manuscript Collection–Columbia)

windowsill. When they awoke the next morning, their shoes were filled with candy, fruit, and cookies.

The Germans contributed to life in the United States in many other ways as well. They established schools throughout the state, including schools for girls. These included elementary and high schools and seminaries. Many taught students in both English and German, at least during the nineteenth century, and for much longer in some small towns. Germans brought with them the concept of kindergartens, and started the first ones in the United States. Often schools were founded by church groups, Catholic and Protestant alike.

German churches and religious organizations contributed much to life in Missouri. The Missouri Synod of the Lutheran Church has become one of the most influential religious organizations in the country. Religious organizations and individuals provided many community services. They provided teachers for the schools, and nurses and aids for hospitals. The Sisters of Mary, for example, came to Missouri in 1872. They built hospitals in St. Louis, St. Charles, and Chillicothe. The sisters served people through epidemics and other disasters, often losing their own lives in the effort.

In more recent years, groups descended from earlier German immigrants have arrived in the state. After World War II, Mennonites and Old Order Amish began settling in areas of the Midwest, including Missouri, where large enough areas of land were available to establish new communities. There had been some Amish settlements in the state in the previous century, but most had died out. These new communities are primarily agricultural. They have maintained their traditional music and stories, and continue to use their local Swiss and German dialects. Their horse-drawn buggies are a common sight on rural roads in several parts of the state.

The cultural life of Missouri today still bears some obvious ties with German culture. German festivals are a regular part of life in the state. St. Louis has its *Strassenfest,* Hermann its *Maifest* and *Oktoberfest*; Concordia has *Wunderbar* Days, and both Concordia and Cole Camp have revived a *Plattdeutsch* theater. Many towns maintain sister-city relationships with German towns important to the history of their Missouri descendants.

These include New Haven's relationship with Borgholzhausen and Westphalia's with Jette Bruns's hometown of Oelde. Many Missourians claim a German heritage. In the 1990 census more than 36 percent reported some German ancestry. The next largest groups are those reporting Irish ancestry (20 percent) and English (14 percent).

The Missouri Department of Natural Resources maintains the Deutschheim State Historic Site in Hermann. Its purpose is to preserve and study German immigrant history and culture. The site includes three houses, two of which are open to the public, gardens, furniture, and other items used in daily life, as well as special exhibits.

The German immigrants lie buried in the cemeteries on hillsides in Westphalia, Hermann, St. Charles, and St. Louis. They are gone, but their traditions are not. Many Americans eat sausages, drink beer and wine, decorate Christmas trees, and have children who attend kindergartens. The German immigrants came with dreams of a better life for their own children. The lives we live are a result of those dreams.

For More Reading

The Arts and Architecture of German Settlements in Missouri: A Survey of Vanishing Culture, by Charles van Ravenswaay (Columbia: University of Missouri Press, 1977), contains a wealth of information and excellent photographs of German American buildings, furniture, and other items. It shows the wide variety of German American craft and decorative arts.

Contented among Strangers: Rural German-Speaking Women and Their Families in the Nineteenth-Century Midwest, by Linda Schelbitzki Pickle (Urbana and Chicago: University of Illinois Press, 1996), examines the experiences of German immigrant women who settled with their families on midwestern farms or in rural communities and played a central role in preserving their ethnic and cultural identities.

The German-American Experience in Missouri: Essays in Celebration of the Tricentennial of German Immigration to America, 1683–1983, edited by Howard Wight Marshall and James W. Goodrich (Columbia: Missouri Cultural Heritage Center, Publication No. 2, University of Missouri, 1986), gives information on a variety of subjects. Essays discuss German-language newspapers and other language issues, farm life, architecture, and churches.

Germans for a Free Missouri: Translations from the St. Louis Radical Press, 1857–1862, selected and translated by Steven Rowan, with an introduction and commentary by James Neal Primm (Columbia: University of Missouri Press, 1983), provides a glimpse into the political attitudes of many opposed to slavery. It includes articles written by St. Louis Germans in the early days of the Civil War.

The Germans in Missouri, 1900–1918: Prohibition, Neutrality, and Assimilation, by David W. Detjen (Columbia: University of Missouri Press, 1985), includes an excellent chapter on German culture in St. Louis and details the struggles over Prohibition and World War I.

Hermann: The German Settlement Society of Philadelphia and Its Colony Hermann, Missouri, by William G. Bek (reprinted by Historic Hermann, Inc. and published by American Press, Inc., 1984), provides details on the founding and early settlement of the town. The book includes many interesting and sometimes humorous stories from the early days of the town.

Hold Dear as Always: Jette, a German Immigrant Life in Letters, edited by Adolf E. Schroeder and Carla Schulz-Geisberg (Columbia: University of Missouri Press, 1988), illustrates the difficulties faced by German women who settled in frontier Missouri. It includes an excellent introduction by the editor, Jette's autobiography, and many letters to family members in Germany. In these letters she allows her feelings of joy, sadness, and frustration to show clearly.

Immigrants in the Ozarks: A Study in Ethnic Geography, by Russel L. Gerlach (Columbia: University of Missouri Press, 1976), includes a chapter on the Germans in Missouri that discusses their attitudes toward religion, language, and temperance. It provides an interesting contrast with the attitudes of other early settlers in the state, particularly the English and Scotch-Irish.

News from the Land of Freedom: German Immigrants Write Home, edited by Walter D. Kamphoefner, Wolfgang Helbich, and Ulrike Sommer (Ithaca, N.Y.: Cornell University Press, 1991), contains letters written by German immigrants, including some in Missouri, describing for their friends and families in Germany the new life they found. These letters show how attractive America sounded to those still in Germany.

St. Louis Germans, 1850–1920: The Nature of an Immigrant Community and Its Relation to the Assimilation Process, by Audrey L. Olson (New York: Arno Press, 1980), provides interesting information about the German community in St. Louis. Because it covers such a long period of time, it presents a fairly complete discussion of change in the St. Louis German community. Earlier Olson had published an article on the same topic called "The Nature of an Immigrant Community" (*Missouri Historical Review* 66 [1972]: 342–59).

"Stereotypes and Reality: Nineteenth Century German Women in Missouri," by Linda Pickle (*Missouri Historical Review* 79

[1985]: 291–312), discusses the stereotypes and realities of the lives of German women on the Missouri frontier. The article examines the hardships facing these women in adjusting to a new world and dealing with old prejudices.

The Uncorrupted Heart: Journals and Letters of Frederick Julius Gustorf, 1800–1845, edited by Fred Gustorf (Columbia: University of Missouri Press, 1969), includes Frederick Gustorf's impressions of early German settlements in Missouri. Gustorf's observations are often critical of both Americans and other German immigrants. The journals show how the attitudes of one class toward another divided the German immigrant community in America.

The Westfalians: From Germany to Missouri, by Walter D. Kamphoefner (Princeton, N.J.: Princeton University Press, 1987), is a scholarly book that focuses on the German immigrants who settled in St. Charles and Warren counties, including an excellent discussion of the reasons for emigration.

William G. Bek also published a series of articles on "The Followers of Duden" that appeared in the *Missouri Historical Review* beginning in 1919. This series contains translations from the writings of Muench, Goebel, Steines, and others.

Many excellent sources of information containing a great amount of detail on the lives of the Germans in Missouri can be found among the numerous local and county histories published since the arrival of the first immigrants.

Der Maibaum, a quarterly publication of the Deutschheim Association, includes articles and illustrations on both current activities and historical subjects. Issues are available through the Association, P.O. Box 16, Hermann, MO 65041.

The Western Historical Manuscript Collection at the University of Missouri includes many unpublished works including letters, memoirs, diaries, and interviews. Many of these have been translated into English, and typed copies are available. These documents may be obtained through any of the four University of Missouri campus Western Historical Manuscript Collections.

Index

About the Authors

Robyn Burnett and Ken Luebbering enjoying a cold drink in the White Stone Inn in Rich Fountain. The restaurant is located in a restored nineteenth-century general mercantile building. (Photograph by Sam Schnieders)

Ken Luebbering was born into a family of Missouri Germans more than one hundred years after some of his ancestors emigrated. His was the first generation in the family to speak English as a first language. He is a writer and professor of English at Lincoln University in Jefferson City, Missouri.

Robyn Burnett's immigrant ancestors came primarily from the British Isles, but one of her great-grandmothers was Pennsylvania Dutch. Robyn is a budget and policy analyst for the Missouri Department of Health and a freelance writer.